HISTORY OF HORSERACING

DAVID MYERS

CONTENTS

This edition first published in the UK in 2006 by Green Umbrella Publishing exclusively for: Sutton Publishing, Phoenix Mill, Thrupp, Stroud, Gloucestershire GL5 2BU

First published in the UK 2006

British Library Cataloguing in Publication Data.
A catalogue record of this book is available from the British Library.

Printed and bound in Singapore

ISBN 0 7509 4694 6

CONTENTS

Right
Chariot racing in 50 BC.

The racing of horses has as long a history as any sport. Almost as soon as the horse had been domesticated it was only natural that man wanted to see which was the fastest animal. There are records of the Ancient Greeks taking part in just such an activity, and while the first Olympics in 776 BC did not feature horse racing, within a hundred years four-horse chariot racing had become an event in the Games.

Various other forms of equine sport developed during the next two hundred years. Bareback riding contests, mule-cart racing and events confined to male or female horses came to the fore. These contests often involved chariots and they formed the basis of the sport until the Middle Ages. By then, horse racing had spread right across Europe and the East.

It was reported as early as 1 AD that chariots were being used in Britain and Ireland, where races were staged at the Curragh, a venue that still hosts major race meetings.

In Great Britain the earliest recorded horse race took place at Netherby, near York, around 210 AD, when it was reported

CHAPTER 1
THE ORIGINS AND DEVELOPMENT

that the Roman emperor Septimus Alexander was closely involved with the event. In Henry II's reign racing took place at Smithfield in London, an area that was later to become known for its meat market, and by the time of Richard I (1157-1199) the sport had become fashionable.

It could be said that the birth of modern horse racing took place when English knights returned from foreign shores with speedier Arabian horses. It took many years for Europeans to learn about Eastern horses, with the result that faster animals became the norm, and races were beginning to be staged in countries such as Italy and France.

There is living evidence of racing in Medieval Italy in the form of the annual event in Siena – Il Palio. The course is the town square, the Piazza del Campo, where ten horses ridden by jockeys sporting the colours and emblems of a particular district of the city (the contrade) race around a tight track at breakneck speed. The culmination of Il Palio, the race itself, lasts for not much longer than a minute and a half. The preparations, however, go on for days so that the event becomes a great festival of colour and excitement.

Back in Britain, horses were being bred for specific purposes, such as agriculture, military activities, and racing.

It was the Arabian stallions that were producing better quality horses, displaying both speed and stamina. It was also at this time that races, or matches, took place. Owners would arrange such contests with the sole purpose of settling arguments, and usually large wagers, centred on the identity of the faster horse. These races became a popular activity for the rich and noble, with one of the first records of such a race occurring in 1377, when the Prince of Wales, shortly to be crowned as Richard II, competed against the Earl of Arundel.

The sixteenth century saw the first official racecourse open in Britain at Chester in 1540, where horses raced for the first prize of a silver bell.

During the next one hundred years more race meetings took place at various locations across Britain such as Carlisle, Doncaster, Lanark, Liverpool, Newmarket, Salisbury and York. During this era the foundations of a long-standing relationship between the Royal Family and horse racing were laid. In 1575 Elizabeth I built a new Royal Stud in Staffordshire, and there were races in the time of James I (1603-1625) at Hampton Court, Tutbury, Eltham and Cole Park with silver and golden bells the prizes for there was no money attached to racing apart from personal wagers. In 1625 when Charles I acceded to the throne, he had a palace and stables built at Newmarket.

The development of the modern thoroughbred racehorse came about in the mid-seventeenth century during the reign of Charles II, who was the Royal Patron of the Turf. Imported purebred Arabians, the closely related Turkish and Barbary sires, covered the mixed-bred British mares, so that all modern thoroughbreds can be traced back to these sires – known as the 'founding sires' – the Byerley Turk (born approximately in 1680), the Darley Arabian (1700), and the Godolphin Arabian (1724). It was also during this period in history that the first racetrack appeared in North America, on Long Island (New York) in 1665.

Above
Darley Arabian, 1720.

The eighteenth century was one of the most important in the sport's history and the developments that took place then had a major influence on the future of horse racing in Britain. At the start of the century, in the reign of Queen Anne (1702-1714), horse racing became a professional sport, with races involving several thoroughbreds, replacing matches between two horses.

As the popularity for horseracing grew, and with prize money increasing, there was a call for an authority to take control of the sport. In 1752, a group of rich, influential racing enthusiasts formed the Jockey Club. This organisation compiled the first set of rules for horse racing, and authorised racecourses to host meetings under these guidelines and restrictions.

There are two main codes of horse racing that have dominated in Britain over the past five hundred years, namely the Flat and National Hunt. The Flat has always been viewed as a rich man's sport, designed for the flashier horses with impeccable bloodlines. National Hunt, meanwhile, is regarded as proper racing by virtue of sorting the men from the boys, both in equine and human terms, where only the bravest need apply.

Flat racing is suited to the smaller, agile thoroughbred blessed with more speed, rather than the stamina seen in hunters in National Hunt racing. Thoroughbred horses on the Flat race over distances split into four categories. The fastest type runs over sprint distances, between five and six furlongs, while those with slightly less speed will race between seven furlongs to a mile. The next category of Flat horse is referred to as a middle-distance type, covering distances of a mile-and-a-quarter to a mile-and-a-half, the distance of the Derby. The final batch of runners on the Flat are known as the stayers, racing over distances from a mile-and-three-quarters to a maximum distance of two-and three-quarter miles.

Above
Godolphin Arabian, 1740.

Below
Contestants take part in an early Steeplechase in the 18th Century.

The first recorded steeplechase took place in Ireland during 1752. The name was taken from the visible landmarks to which they raced, and according to tradition, the first steeplechase was run between Buttevant Church and Saint Mary's Doneraile, otherwise known as the St. Leger steeple, in County Limerick. Over a distance slightly further than that of the Grand National – four-and-a-half miles – two Irish foxhunters O'Calloghan and Blake set off to see who possessed the fastest horse. This match saw both horses tackle severe obstacles unseen in the modern sport, including tree logs and stone walls, racing through deep water, down slopes, across open farmland, up and down dipping lanes, and dodging low trees.

Horses used for foxhunting became faster towards the end of the eighteenth century, as they were bred more for speed in order to keep up with the lightweight hounds. The art of jumping was still as significant as speed due to the natural landscape of the countryside used for cross-country matches in that period, and in 1790, the first race involving more than two horses took place in Leicestershire.

Steeplechasing in the nineteenth century became more popular, with bigger races appearing, such as the St Albans chase in 1830. Nine years later, the first official running of the Grand National took place although the race had been run for three years unofficially beforehand and all roads leading to Aintree were jammed on the morning of the race even then.

Despite being a hit with the public, steeplechase fixtures were not as popular with the press who were of the view that wrongdoings took place at such gatherings, including brawling and cock fighting. This was probably true of the smaller meetings that were badly organised and were without rules, being unrecognised by the Jockey Club. Steeple chasing was heading in the wrong direction towards the second-half of the nineteenth century, until owner-rider, Fothergill Rowlands, who had sacrificed his career as a doctor for racing, set up a series of a dozen races, including one at Market Harborough in 1860. These valuable races were strictly controlled and led to a set of rules known as 'The Harborough Act', before the National Hunt Committee was formed by The Jockey Club in 1865.

The first list of colours had been introduced by the Jockey Club in 1762, so owners could identify their horses during a race. This first list of colours included seventeen individual sets to be shared amongst owners. In 1766 the first auction sales for thoroughbreds were held. Richard Tattersall, who was one of the first thoroughbred breeders to sell his stock, founded these auctions and some of the early sales took place in the heart of London at Hyde Park Corner. The Tattersall sales remained in London until 1977, when the operation moved to Newmarket. In Europe, the sport was developing along parallel lines. In 1776 Plaine des Sablons, near Paris, was the first racecourse to be built in France.

Meanwhile, in England, the first races restricted to two-year-olds were being planned, along with a series of races for the best three-year-olds, later to become known as the

Above
A cartoon depiction of an early Tattersall sale.

Classics. Prior to this, the most prestigious races were the "King's Plates", a series of races run over four miles, in which horses had to carry the welter-weight burden of 12 stone – not dissimilar to today's Grand National.

The first of these Classics to take place was the St. Leger in 1776 at Cantley Common, Doncaster over a distance of one mile six furlongs and 132 yards. It was not until 1779 that the second Classic was introduced. This was the Oaks, for three-year-old fillies only and run over a mile-and-a-half on Epsom Downs. A year later, the third Classic was run over the same course, but the Derby was open to both colts and fillies, and run over a mile. The distance was extended to fall in line with that of the Oaks – a mile-and-a-half – five years later.

The next two Classics to complete the set of five did not appear until the next century. In 1809 the Two Thousand Guineas was first run over a mile for three-year-old colts and fillies at Newmarket, and then five years later came the One Thousand Guineas, for fillies only. Run over the same distance as the Two Thousand Guineas, this race completed the list of Classics, still the biggest races on the Flat in Britain.

The nineteenth century was also a time when modern horse racing developed worldwide, with Australia staging its first race fixture at Hyde Park in Sydney in 1810. Five years later, South Africa formed its own Jockey Club and racing got underway at Green Point Common near Cape Town. Germany became a horse racing country in 1822, but modern horse racing was not to reach the Far East until 1862, with the first Japanese racetrack opening at Yokohama. In Britain, Sandown Park became the first enclosed course in 1875, and the entrance fees charged enabled the venue to offer bigger prize-money than elsewhere.

It was also around the same period, in the 1870s and 1880s, that hurdle racing gathered momentum, with the Grand International Hurdle at Croydon racecourse becoming one of

Above
The St. Leger race from 1842, the oldest 'classic'.

the first major races. Racing over hurdles, however, had been recorded as early as 1821 in Bristol, and some smaller obstacles also featured in the early years of the Grand National. They did not catch on in their own right until the late nineteenth century when these smaller hurdles were introduced for the faster thoroughbreds to race, while acknowledging their inability to handle the bigger fences.

At the turn of the twentieth century the breeding of thoroughbreds in Britain changed with the import of sires from America. The twentieth century also brought with it an array of technological innovations that were to benefit the horseracing world. In 1947, the first camera was used at a racetrack to determine the outcome of a race. This event took place at the start of the Flat season at Epsom Downs, when a photo finish identified the correct placings in the Great Metropolitan Handicap on April 22. The first time a photo finish was used to decide the outcome of a Classic race came on April 27 1949 in the Two Thousand Guineas at Newmarket.

National Hunt's profile began to match that of the Flat after the turn of the twentieth century, with major meetings taking place at Cheltenham from 1902, along with bigger races such as the Gold Cup and Champion Hurdle. The progress that National Hunt was making led to an increase in point-to-point fixtures. They had first taken place back in 1836 and the popularity of point-to-point racing

Engraved by P Roberts, from a Miniature Painted by R.Cosway Esq.r R.A.
Col.l St.t Leger

Left
General John Haves St. Leger, who founded the St. Leger classic horse race.

Below
West Australian who was the first horse to win the Triple Crown consisting of the Two Thousand Guineas, the Derby, and the St. Leger, 1853.

Above
Workmen trimming the 'chair' jump at Aintree, 1937.

Above right
Starting stall at Newmarket, 1965 .

Right
Harness racing at Alexandra Park, New Zealand 2005.

Far right
Southwell racecourse, which offers an all-weather sand track.

grew in the 1870s as amateur huntsmen were omitted from National Hunt racing, but could still participate in these races run from one point, or steeple, to another.

The Master of Hounds Point-to-Point Association introduced their own set of rules in 1913, allowing for the inclusion of lady riders, but excluded professional jockeys from the National Hunt circuit. This form of racing is still very popular today, allowing stable lads to participate, and can often present a future National Hunt runner with its first opening. As a result, these point-to-point fixtures, mainly at small countryside venues are usually well attended, not only by the public but also by trainers and owners from the National Hunt arena, scouting for any future stars with jumping ability.

1950 saw races being timed accurately for the first time, and then two years later, Goodwood provided the first racecourse commentary.

Sandwiched between these dates in 1948, horse racing became projected to a much wider audience in Britain when the BBC broke new ground in televising a steeplechase from Sandown Park. Starting stalls were first used in this country in July 1965 at Newmarket.

In 1989, the first all-weather track was installed in Britain at Southwell racecourse. The introduction of this form of racing on sand offered benefits to the sport, giving Flat trainers the option of running their horses during the winter as the surface was able to survive freezing conditions. This style of racing on sand was based on dirt racing held in America, and now all-weather racing stages its own Derby every March at the end of the winter season, recently given Pattern status as a Group 3 event. Two more all-weather tracks followed, with Lingfield in Surrey and Wolverhampton in the Midlands both staging numerous fixtures as this form of racing proved increasingly popular.

Another form of racing staged in America, but yet to be taken up seriously in this country, is harness racing. It also features in countries such as Australia, Canada and New Zealand. This type of racing allows horses to trot, rather than gallop, pulling two-wheeled carts with jockeys called sulkies. The majority of horses seen in this sphere, are standardbred in comparison to the thoroughbreds of conventional horse racing, with shorter legs and longer bodies well-suited to harness racing. It is perhaps not such a long way from the chariot races that were seen in the early Olympics.

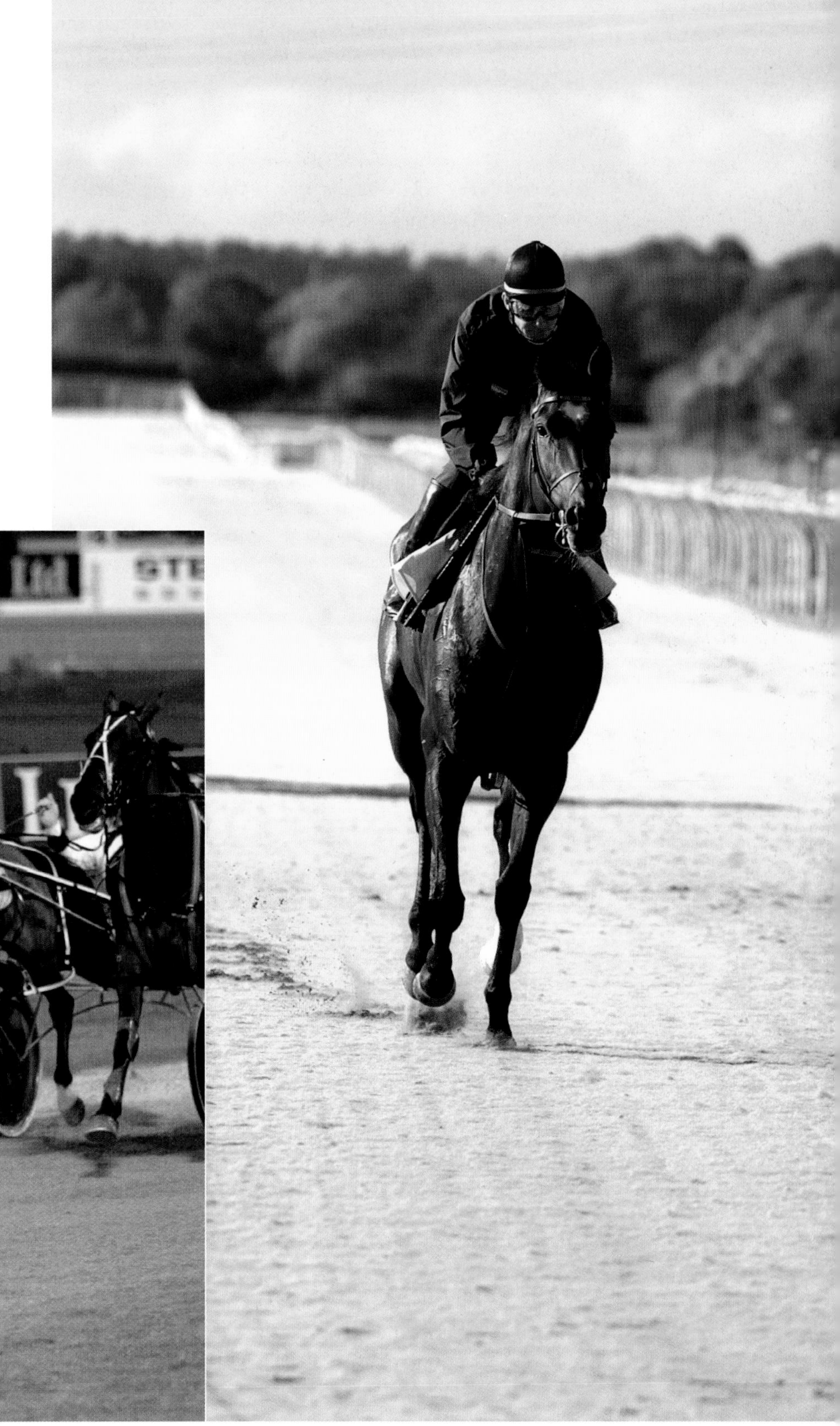

CHAPTER 2
ADMINISTRATION

Before the mid-eighteenth century horseracing was devoid of any governing body. Until then, races, or 'matches' between horses were subject to all sorts of corruption and malpractice, and rules were non-existent. It was a disreputable state of affairs that something had to be done if the sport was to have any credibility, so the Jockey Club was formed in 1750.

This club was made up of rich, influential racing enthusiasts who met for the first time at the Star and Garter Inn, the south side inn of the two in Pall Mall, London. The Jockey Club was not only a means of controlling racing but was also a venue in which prominent owners could meet to arrange races between their horses. Two years later, a race was run at Newmarket for owners of the Jockey Club, before that authority gradually acquired land in the Suffolk area, including an area used for further gatherings known as "The Coffee Room".

The administration and organisation of horse racing was at first a straightforward enough task for those controlling it, with only a handful of racecourses to manage and a rigid set of rules firmly in place. But, as the popularity of racing grew, the club began employing outsiders to cover specialist areas, and in 1770 they hired entrepreneur James Weatherby as a secretary, who along with his nephew, took control of the club's business.

Below
George Bentinck, one of the original members of the Jockey Club.

In 1791, Weatherby's published the General Stud Book, detailing the pedigree record of approximately 400 horses that were at the foundation of all thoroughbred stock worldwide. Weatherby's remained in London for 200 years before moving out to Wellinborough in Northamptonshire in the late 1960s, where they currently employ a workforce of 350 people.

The tasks covered by the Weatherby's team include some of the most important administrative services to horse racing. They include the racing calendar featuring all races with conditions on a weekly basis, the registration of ownership, of colours, of horse names, and horses in training. Weatherby's also receive all race entries and declarations, produce the race cards including the allocation of weights, store all the official handicap ratings of horses, conduct the draw, divide races, as well as collecting and distributing the prize money for all British races.

Since taking the significant step of employing James Weatherby in 1770, the Jockey Club has been responsible for many other notable changes in its 250-year history. Racing colours worn by jockeys became compulsory in 1762, and the first official judge was appointed in 1772. A year later, the Racing Calendar first appeared and in 1791 the first handicap race was run – the Oatlands Stakes at Ascot.

Between 1768 and 1830 the club had amongst its members Sir Charles Bunbury and Lord George Bentinck, both of who were senior stewards, before appointing Admiral Rous in 1855. The latter was the official handicapper who gave birth to the weight-for-age-scale, and these three figures were known as the "Dictators of the Turf", laying the foundations for the multi-million pound industry in existence today.

As the Jockey Club increasingly took control of Newmarket Heath, it grew in stature. Its rules and orders were obeyed not just in Newmarket, but also by the stewards of other meetings. It was then agreed that any racecourse accepting these rules would forward any disputes for adjudication to the Jockey Club. The club stewards were given the power to take disciplinary action against anyone in breach of the rules, including the suspension and banning of jockeys.

The stewards' role at a racecourse has evolved to form part of an on-course team consisting of skilled individuals who must all be present before racing can get underway. This team should include a clerk of the course,

a clerk of the scales, a starter, a judge, a veterinary surgeon, a doctor and ambulance.

In 1833 a meeting held by the Jockey Club decided that all horses in Newmarket should take their ages from January 1, instead of May 1, a rule that was adopted by all other racecourses 25 years later. More important decisions were made over the years, and in 1879 women jockeys were licensed for the first time, before number cloths were introduced in 1920.

The mid-sixties were also significant in the authority's history for in 1965 starting stalls for Flat racing were introduced at Newmarket. A year later, as a result of a court case, the Jockey Club was forced into issuing trainers' licences to women, before welcoming females as members of its organisation 11 years later.

In recent years, from 1993 to 2006, the Jockey Club has handed over a share of its responsibilities to the newly formed British Horseracing Board, and the Horseracing Regulatory Authority. The

Above
Newmarket in 1790, where owners of the Jockey Club held their early races.

Left
The Star and Garter Inn, where first meetings of the Jockey Club took place.

Right
Ascot in the 19th century, which hosted the first handicap race, the Oaklands Stakes.

Far right
A woman jockey, pictured in 1926. They were licensed for the first time in 1879.

Below far right
Handmade spats are applied to 'Gold Pot', at the Jockey Club 1935.

BHB helped introduce Sunday racing with betting in 1995, the same year National Hunt racing appeared during the summer months to make it an all-year-round sport.

The Jockey Club now takes more of a back seat in its involvement within the racing industry, although it is still responsible for 13 racecourses in the United Kingdom, through the Racecourse Holdings Trust. It is also responsible for the Jockey Club Estates who manage over 4,000 acres of land at Newmarket, including both Newmarket racecourses, the Jockey Club Rooms, the National Stud land and the National Horseracing Museum. Racing Welfare is another company looked after by the Jockey Club, offering support and funds for injured jockeys and stable staff.

The number of different bodies now involved in racing has made it more difficult for all parties to agree on a particular agenda, especially matters regarding the future funding of the sport. When betting shops were legalised in 1961, turnover figures from racecourse attendances dropped, leading to the formation of the Horserace Betting Levy Board. This statutory body was given the job of not only raising a levy from bookmakers and the Tote, but also making sure funds were allocated to the right avenues within the horse racing industry. These funds all contribute towards the cost of particular areas of racing, such as financing over 50 per cent of all prize-money at racecourses, track improvements including equipment such as photo-finish cameras, doping laboratories, investment in home bred stallions, and equine research.

Other associations with input and influence in the horse racing industry include the Racecourse Association, the trade body representing 58 of Britain's racecourses. Then there is the Racehorse Owners Association that promotes and protects the owners along with contributing towards the financial structure of British racing. Other relevant organisations include the National Trainers Federation which does the same job for the trainers by liaising with other bodies to help plan racing, while the British School of Racing provides training for people employed in horse racing.

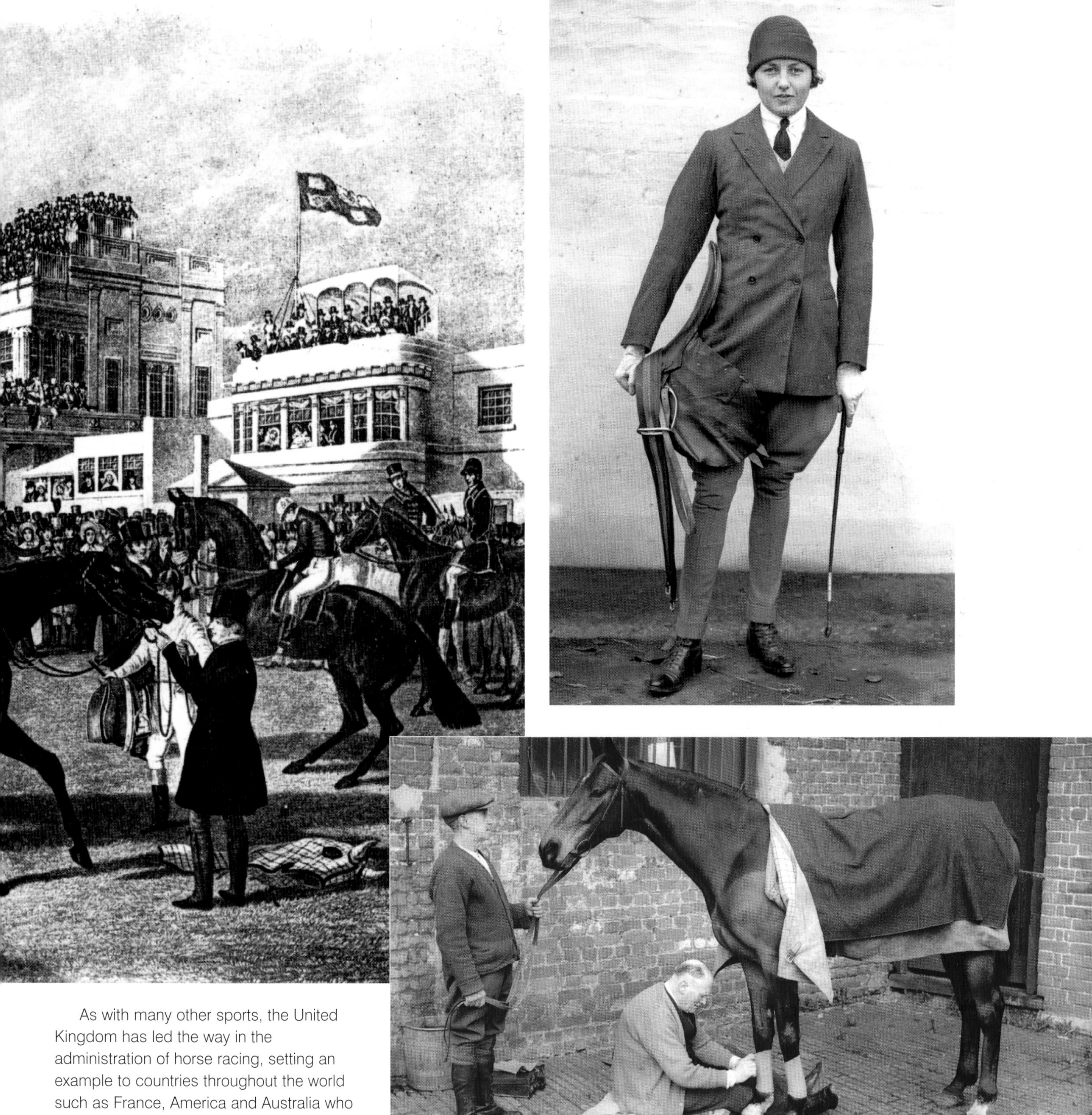

As with many other sports, the United Kingdom has led the way in the administration of horse racing, setting an example to countries throughout the world such as France, America and Australia who have all duplicated the system, each having its own version of the Jockey Club.

CHAPTER 3
GREAT JOCKEYS

Right
Steve Donoghue being weighed before a race, 1930.

Below left
Fred Archer, one of the greatest jockeys of the nineteenth century.

Below right
Champion jockey Sir Gordon Richards at the stables in 1947.

Throughout the history of the sport a jockey has needed many attributes – balance, bravery, composure, timing, strength, rhythm, desire, touch – to reach the top. This has always been the case, and those who have made an impression in the sport from the earliest days have all been able to point to these qualities.

Despite this assertion, the early jockeys tended to be somewhat anonymous figures who did not command too much attention. This was not surprising as they were regarded as simply hired hands, paid to perform a function for the owners. That is why some of the early Champions have failed to make much of a mark in history. They deserved to gain attention, but in the days before sportsmen became celebrities, they were thought of as being unimportant in the general scheme of things. The trainers had some notable skills and the owners, with their financial clout that made it all possible certainly deserved recognition in the social climate of the day. Jockeys were mere pilots who accompanied the horse to glory.

That is why little is known of the early Champion Jockeys when the likes of Elnathan Flatman and George Fordham featured so prominently in the role of honour. Flatman, for example, won the title for the first 13 years of its existence from 1840. Fordham took over in 1855 and won the title for the next nine years and won again, or shared the honour, five times in the subsequent seven years.

In 1874 Fred Archer won the first of his 13 consecutive Champion Jockey titles, and he was the man who could be said to have begun the recognition of jockeys and as integral part of the team that deserves credit for a winner. Even so, his tragic story illustrates how little heed was paid to the jockey in those days.

Archer rode 2,748 winners from 8,084 rides between 1869 and 1886. The first of those winners came over the jumps on a minor card at Bangor when he was just 12 years of age and weighed only four stone 11 pounds. From those humble beginnings, he went on to partner 21 Classic winners, with five Derby successes among them. He was a hard man with victory meaning everything to him. Nobody could stand between him and a winner, including his brother who he is reputed to have once dumped over the rails as he went for glory.

But all this took its toll and the continual battle with the scales, in which he was not alone, was a contributory factor in damaging his body and turning his mind. He had to fight particularly hard to make the weight for the 1886 Cambridgeshire. He contracted typhoid fever followed by a severe bout of depression during which he shot himself. He was not yet 30 years of age.

Steve Donoghue was the next man to dominate the Championship with ten consecutive titles from 1914 to stake his claim as one of the all-time greats. Born in Warrington, Donoghue had his first winner in France when he was 14 years of age. He rode in Ireland as well, but in 1911 he returned to England to ride for trainer Henry Persse with conspicuous success.

He could boast six Derby wins and three of the other four Classics, but he completed the set in 1937 when he won the One Thousand Guineas on Exhibitionist. He retired from the saddle that year to take up training and breeding to continue working with the thoroughbreds that he referred to as his "best friends" but without the success that he enjoyed as a jockey. He died of heart failure in 1945.

From a statistical viewpoint, Gordon Richards was the greatest British jockey of all time. After riding ponies from an early age, he became a stable lad at fifteen in 1919 before riding his

first winner a year later. In 1925 Richards won the Jockey Championship with 118 winners in his first full season for the first of 26 titles in 29 years.

Four of the five English Classics were added to his impressive record in the following years, but he struggled to win the Epsom Derby in 27 attempts before his big year in 1953. Unbeknown to him at the time, this was to be his final ride in the great race, and he managed to complete the full-set of Classics when coming home on the Queen's Pinza to rapturous applause in Coronation year. Richards had become the first jockey to be knighted earlier in the week, and the Queen was there to greet him in the winner's enclosure. However, Sir Gordon was less fortunate the following year when suffering an injury to his pelvis, causing him to retire from the saddle. His final total of winners stood at 4,870 – a record that stands to this day.

Doug Smith took over as Champion Jockey from Richards, winning the title five times, and Australian Scobie Breasley won four prior to the emergence of Lester Piggott as the dominant jockey. Piggott won the first of his 11 titles in 1960 and the last in 1982, with an impressive set of statistics in between. He rode the first of his 4,493 winners at the age of 12 and soon made a reputation for himself as a raw teenager, despite being unusually tall for a jockey at five foot eight inches, and won the first of his 30 British Classics in 1954, aged eighteen.

Above
The 1949 Ascot Gold Cup with Alycidon, ridden by Doug Smith.

Left
Lester Piggott is led in on the race winner Never Say Die, at the 1954 Epsom Derby.

That milestone was to be just one of many achieved by Piggott. He rode nine Derby winners, had three Arc triumphs, to say nothing of 25 centuries (a hundred winners in a season), while he found time in his frantically busy schedule to ride 38 Classic winners abroad. His popularity throughout the sixties and seventies earned him yet another title as the housewives' favourite, such was his reliability to do the job. Yet, despite all the winners in his prime, it was the latter part of his life that caused the biggest headlines.

After retiring as a jockey in 1985, he had a brief spell as a trainer, before being gaoled for tax irregularities in 1987 and losing his OBE. However, he returned to the saddle in 1990 to win the Breeders' Cup Mile in America on Royal Academy,

Above
Willie Carson pictured in jovial mood in 1992.

Right
Pat Eddery (left) at Newmarket, 2003.

Far right
Joe Mercer in relaxed mood before a race.

causing a ripple throughout the horseracing world for Piggott was 54 at the time. There was more to come, though, as he rode the winner of the Two Thousand Guineas on Rodrigo De Triano two years later, before retiring for the second and final time in 1995.

Joe Mercer landed another blow for the senior generation when he took the title in 1979 at the age of 45, while it was won by the likes of other outstanding jockeys such as Willie Carson (with 3,828 career wins from 1959-1996), Pat Eddery (with 4,632 career wins from 1969-2003, before taking out a

trainers licence in 2005) and the American Steve Cauthen. They took the title for a number of years in the 1970s and 80s before another of the greats emerged in the shape of Frankie (or Lianfranco to give him his full name) Dettori.

This popular Italian has become one of the most famous jockeys in Britain since Lester Piggott. Dettori arrived in Britain during the mid-eighties, when he became Champion apprentice in 1989 before establishing himself as one of the greatest jockeys of that generation. He was employed by the powerful Godolphin yard, for whom he has ridden a bagful of Group One victories, most of which were celebrated by his trademark flying dismount, including four of the five English Classics. The only race to have eluded him is the Derby, but it is hard to imagine that this son of a jockey back in Italy will remain with that omission as a blot on his record.

However, Dettori achieved one feat that may never be repeated and which rocketed him to a super-stardom unknown to his early predecessors. On 28th September 1996 he rode every winner on the seven-race card at Ascot, costing bookmakers millions, as punters across the land poured more money on him as they day unfolded and the sporting world stopped to witness a unique moment.

By 2005, Dettori had three Champion Jockey titles to his credit, while one of the most controversial jockeys in recent years, Kieren Fallon, had six along with a clean sweep of Classics apart from the St. Leger. Against his successes go a strongly-denied allegation of race-fixing, time spent in a drying-out clinic, very public splits with trainers Henry Cecil and Sir Michael Stoute and an incident in 1994 when he was banned for six months after being accused of pulling a fellow jockey from his horse at Beverley. It is hoped that such a talented horseman will be remembered for his ability rather than his shortcomings.

Other top jockey's have come from abroad, as well as those already mentioned. Bill Shoemaker from the United States was destined for a career in the saddle with a name like that and a birth weight of just two and a half pounds.

He piloted his first winner home a month after his opening ride in 1949, creating a distinct impression with fellow jockeys.

Left
Frankie Dettori leaps in delight after winning the Queen Elizabeth II stakes during his seven race win at Ascot, 1996.

Above left
Kieren Fallon celebrates after winning The Derby at Epsom, 2004.

Above right
Willie Shoemaker at the races, 1984.

He was awarded the George Woolf Memorial trophy by his peers just two years after making his debut. In 1955, Shoemaker won the first of his 11 Triple Crown races, when landing the Kentucky Derby on Swaps, a race he was to win on another four occasions. His final victory in that event, on Ferdinand in 1986, saw him become the oldest jockey to win it, aged 54.

It was his level of fitness that enabled him to ride until he was 58 when he rode the last of his 8,833 winners at Gulfstream Park in 1990 before participating in his last race just two weeks later. A year after that he was tragically paralysed in a car accident, but that did not prevent him from training 90 winners from his wheelchair, including 13 graded stakes winners. "The Shoe", who stood at less than five foot, was described in his prime as, pound-for pound, the best athlete alive.

Also in the United States of America, Julie Krone stands as the leading woman jockey with over 3,500 career wins from 1981, whilst Gary Stevens accumulated 4,512 winning rides from 1979 until retiring in the same year as Pat Day who bowed out with 8,803 career wins between 1973 and 2005. The latest great American jockey to retire was Jerry Bailey with 5,892 career wins from 1974 to January 2006.

When considering the great jockeys, there is another name that will not be instantly recognised like that of Piggott or Shoemaker, yet Laffit Pincay Junior deserves to be right up there with the best. In fact, it was Shoemaker's world record of 8,833 career winners, which was surpassed by Venezuelan Pincay in 1999. In December that year at Hollywood Park he partnered Irish Nip to notch up winner number 8,834, and he progressed his record to an astonishing total of 9,530 winners before injury forced his retirement in 2003.

Injury is an ever-present worry for any jockey, but it has always been a greater fear for those going over the jumps. A fall is an inherent danger and the resilience of those who earn their living by guiding powerful animals over the obstacles. Furthermore, the rewards are less for the jump jockeys as this branch of the sport has generally been less fashionable than

Above
Jerry Bailey celebrates after winning the Breeders' Cup Classic race, 2005.

Above right
Gary Stevens poses in the winners' circle after the Santa Anita Derby at the Santa Anita Park, 2003.

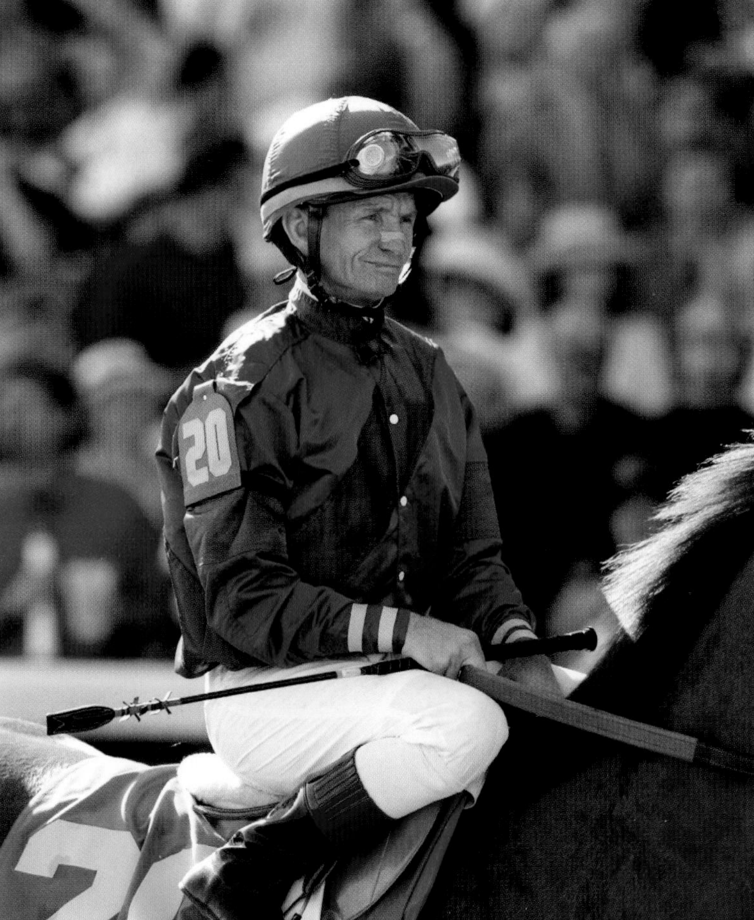

Middle
Julie Krone celebrates winning the Breeders' Cup in 2003.

Left
Pat Day rides Blue Burner at the 128th Kentucky Derby, 2002.

Below
Laffit Pincay Junior walks to the winners circle after a win in 1999.

the Flat, although the sense of achievement and fellowship might be greater.

Whereas the first Champion Flat jockey was named in 1840, it was not until 1900 that the National Hunt Champion Jockey title came into existence. In that year a Mr. H.S. Sidney rode 53 winners, although the title in those days was awarded for performances throughout the year. In 1926 that changed so the Champion was named for the 1925/26 season rather than on a January to December basis.

F. Mason was a dominant figure in the early years, winning from 1901 to 1907 with just one year

when he missed out, while a certain Ernie Piggott took the title in 1910, 1913 and 1915. He was Lester's grandfather. Frederick Bilbo Rees, Billy Stott and Gerry Wilson all had several years as Champion between the wars, with Rees being the first to record a hundred winners in 1924. The next man to do so was one of the great names of the sport, Fred Winter, in 1952/53.

Winter, the son of a trainer, won the Champion Jockey title four times and was top trainer a further eight times. In all, he won 923 races and was the only man ever to have triumphed in the Grand National, the Champion Hurdle and the Cheltenham Gold Cup as both a jockey and a trainer. This legend of the turf suffered a stroke 16 years before his death at the age of 77 in 2004 and was confined to a wheelchair for the latter years of his life.

Renowned jockeys like Josh Gifford had 641 winners and Stan Mellor with 1,035 career successes and two and three Championship titles respectively. Terry Biddlecombe was a jovial Gloucestershire farmer who won races and titles before turning to training with his wife, Henrietta Knight. Jonjo O'Neill was right up there with the best before one of the very best came to the fore to take the title on seven occasions.

John Francome topped most efforts with 1,138 career wins from 1970-85 while he took the title seven times. One he shared with Peter Scudamore who had eight titles and 1,678 career wins. Scudamore cast a shadow over most and it was some years before the talented Richard Dunwoody stepped out of it. He was Champion three times between 1992 and 1995 while he rode 1,699 winners throughout his career from 1983-1999.

Perhaps topping them all is Tony McCoy. The Northern Irishman rode his first winner at Thurles in 1992, before registering his first victory in England two years later, and then landing the Jockey Championship for the first time in 1995/96, assisted by his partnership with the great trainer, Martin Pipe. McCoy then went about breaking more records, firstly by winning the most jumps races in a National Hunt season with 253, before recording the fastest ever century in a season, and

also the fastest to record 1000 career wins.

In April 2002, he broke the biggest record of all, beating the legendary Sir Gordon Richards' record of 269 winners in the same season, ending with a remarkable 289. His thirst for victories also saw McCoy become the all time leader of jumps winners, having comfortably passed the 2,000 mark at Wincanton in January 2004. McCoy has won the Champion Jockey title every year since his first in 1995-96 – twelve times – and continually raises the bar, setting targets for himself that may never be overcome by anyone else.

Far left inset
Josh Gifford.

From top left to right
Fred Winter, Richard Dunwoody, Terry Biddlecombe and Henrietta Knight with their horse Best Mate, John Francome and Peter Scudamore.

Left inset
Tony McCoy with the Champion National Hunt jockey trophy, 2006.

CHAPTER 4
GREAT TRAINERS

A horse may have all the ability in the world, but it takes a good trainer to place it in the right race in favourable conditions. Great trainers have always had the skill to recognise talent in an animal from an early stage, and nurture it by means of the correct long-term programme. Knowing the right races for a horse requires an educated scanning of the programme book, although the top men in the field have an encyclopaedic knowledge of it, as well as the patience to wait for the appropriate race.

A sound knowledge of breeding is also required in the make-up of any great trainer, appreciating a thoroughbred's family tree so that the horse can run over its optimum distance. An average trainer might be tempted to run horse without taking account of its suitability for the trip, but such slackness does not exist in a quality handler.

The ability to look after and understand both colts and fillies is another quality needed from a trainer who is going to reach the top, as is the versatility to be successful in both codes, namely on the Flat and over the jumps. Finally, there is a requirement for an eye to detail, a conscientious brain that leaves no stone unturned. Good trainers posses some of these qualities, but a great trainer will hold them all, which is why there have been so few throughout the history of the sport.

Just as with jockeys there is a Champion Trainers title for both the Flat and National Hunt racing, with the former starting in 1896 when A. Hayhoe became the first name to be listed on the roll of honour. The jumping title for trainers did not begin until after the Second World War in 1945/46 when T. Rayson took the laurels. He was succeeded by one of the major names in National Hunt training, Fulke Walwyn. He won five titles, the last of which came in 1963/64.

Like many of the greats in this area of the sport, Walwyn was a successful jockey before he turned to training. He had won the Grand National on Reynoldstown, who had won the previous year under another jockey, but in 1938 Walwyn's riding career was terminated when he fractured his skull for a second time. His training record bears comparison with any: four Gold Cups, one Grand National, two Champion Hurdles, five victories in the King George VI Chase, seven in the Whitbread Gold Cup and seven in the Hennessy Gold Cup.

Fred Rimmell got his name on the list as the leading trainer four times, while Ryan Price managed five. The legendary Fred Winter, whose career is examined in more detail as a jockey, took eight titles, the last of which came only three years before he retired in 1988. Michael Dickinson won the title for the first of five times in 1980/81 but will always be remembered for his feat in the 1983 Cheltenham Gold Cup when he saddled the first five home.

Then a name appears on the list with such regularity that it stands out among all the other greats. Martin Pipe has taken the level of training National Hunt horses to new heights. Located in the West Country, Pipe's Pond House yard operates like no other. His sense of detail is unmatched, with all of his horses meticulously given the five-star treatment. They are regularly blood-tested in their own laboratory, as well as having use of modern training facilities such as an indoor schooling track which teaches horses to jump without a jockey, mechanical horse-walkers aiding younger horses, schooling gallops with five hurdles and five open ditches, a treadmill, a swimming pool, and a solarium.

This son of a bookmaker, and an ex-jockey, first entered the ranks of training in the mid-seventies, and has won nearly all of jump racing's most coveted prizes, although the Cheltenham Cup has eluded him. Numerically, Pipe has raised the bar to an extreme level, and has six times recorded in excess of 200 winners in a single season with the highest being 236 in 2003-04. These vast numbers

Below
Trainer Martin Pipe during a race meeting in 1990.

Left
Lester Piggott in conversation with trainer Ryan Price before riding Sacramento Song at Sandown, 1971.

have contributed towards Pipe winning the training Championship 15 times in 17 years, and it came as something of a surprise when he suddenly handed over the reins to his son in April, 2006.

In the early days of the Flat there are some frequently recurring names that take the eye. A. Taylor took the title 12 times between 1907 and 1925, Frank Butters was a serial winner, as was Fred Darling. Noel Murless won nine times and had 19 Classics successes, and Cecil Boyd-Rochfort was five times the leading trainer. He sent out 13 Classic winners and was knighted in 1968 on his retirement from having been the Royal trainer since 1943. The Queen's trainer, Major Dick Hern, is a name that stands out whenever the best in the business are mentioned. Before he retired in 1997, he had won four Championships and 16 Classics.

Two other Flat trainers currently holding a license are also destined to be mentioned with great men of

Above
Captain Cecil Boyd-Rochfort, trainer of the Queen's horses, with jockey Harry Carr at Lingfield Races, 1955.

Above far right
Her Majesty the Queen watches her horse Chief Yeoman run in The Vodafone Live Handicap Stakes Race at Epsom. Sir Michael Stoute the horses trainer is on her right.

the turf when they do decide to retire. Henry Cecil has been at the top of his trade since 1969, claiming ten Championships and 32 Classic winners. Sir Michael Stoute came from Barbados as a 20-year-old and since 1972 has won seven Championships, has handled 11 Classic winners, including Shergar in the 1981 Derby, Shahrastani in 1986, before his third Derby success was provided by Kris Kin in 2003. His greatest success over jumps came in the Champion Hurdle with Kribensis in 1990.

It is this ability to be successful both on the Flat and over jumps that marks out really special trainers. Vincent O'Brien was recently voted horseracing's greatest trainer of all time, with a record that includes winning every major race in Britain and Ireland.

The Master of Ballydoyle, where he trained, initially handled horses over jumps, enjoying his first big race success with Cottage Rake in the Cheltenham Gold Cup in 1948, a race O'Brien won for the next two years. It was also during this period that he became the first trainer to record a consecutive treble of Champion Hurdles at Cheltenham with Hatton's Grace.

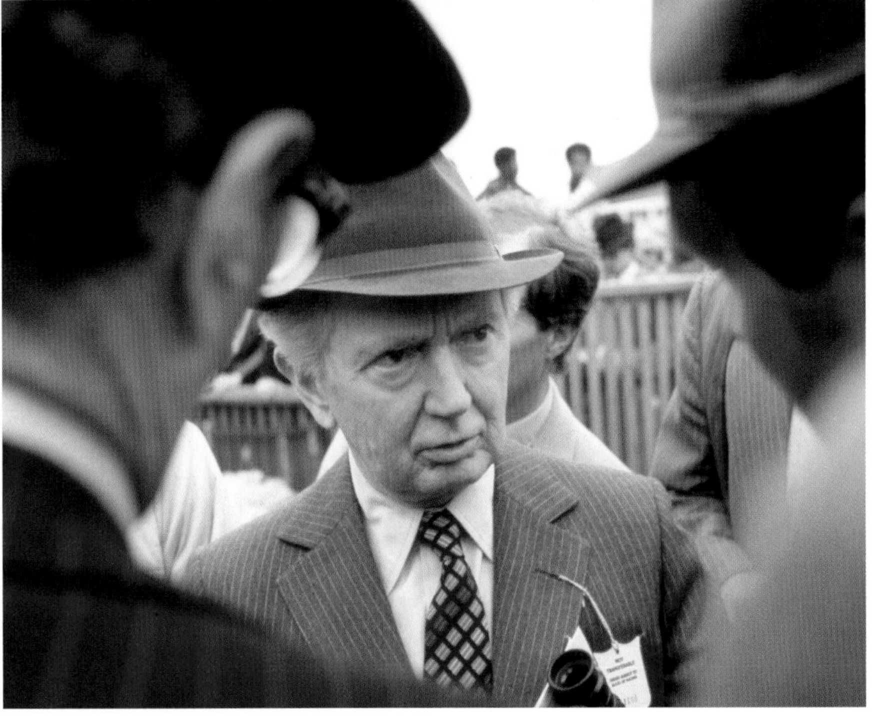

From left to right
Sir Noel Murless receiving his knighthood in 1977, Major Dick Hern, Henry Cecil and Vincent O'Brien meeting the press.

Above
Wayne Lukas, trainer of Kentucky Derby contender Scrimshaw, talks to the media, 2003.

Above right
Kieren Fallon chats to trainer Aidan O'Brien after Gypsy King landed The Dee Stakes Race at Chester Racecourse, 2005.

Next on the National Hunt list for O'Brien was the Grand National, and he did not have to wait long, taking the Aintree event for the first time in 1953 before following up in his customary manner over the following two years, all with different horses. It is a feat that has never been matched.

The next challenge for the Irish genius was to conquer the Flat and Ballymoss got the ball rolling, winning the 1957 St. Leger. A year later, O'Brien crossed the English Channel, to win the first of his three Arc's, and he had the first of his six English Derby successes with Larkspur in 1962.

When he finally retired after 50 years of training, Vincent O'Brien had accumulated 16 English and 27 Irish Classics to go with his triumphs over the jumps. There may never be another trainer to match such feats.

There may never be another trainer to eclipse Vincent O'Brien's achievements, but his namesake is doing a grand job in catching him from the same Ballydoyle premises. After a brief career as a jockey, Aidan O'Brien started training horses over jumps, and managed to win the trainers title during his first season, breaking the prize money record at the same time. The following year he broke the record for winners in a season, before switching over codes to the Flat, just like his predecessor at Ballydoyle.

Predictably, Aidan smashed more records in his first season operating from Ballydoyle, amassing 176 winners over both codes before passing that number the following season. His first major race on the Flat came in 1997, when he sent out the winners of the One Thousand Guineas, Two Thousand Guineas and Derby in his native country. The next two years saw the young genius claim his first English Classic, the Two Thousand Guineas, as well as landing the Champion Hurdle at Cheltenham with the great Istabraq for the first of his three victories.

Aidan O'Brien has since gone from strength to strength, recording some notable achievements, becoming the first overseas handler since Vincent O'Brien to win the leading trainers title in Britain in 2001. The following year, he trained Rock Of Gibraltar to win a world record seven successive Group One races. Although he has taken his foot off the pedal in the National Hunt arena and may not match Vincent O'Brien in that sphere, his age suggests that he has every chance of emulating his namesake over the Flat in the exciting years to come.

Great trainers are not confined to the shores of the British Isles. D. Wayne Lukas has been a legendary American trainer, starting out with success at handling quarter horses for rodeos and shows, with more than 20 Champions, before moving on to make his mark with the thoroughbred racehorse.

Lukas has been even more successful in this field, having consistently set new records including being the first trainer to record over $100 million in prize money, as well as being the first person to win the US Triple Crown with two different horses in the same season – Thunder Gulch & Timber Country in 1995. He is also by far the leading trainer of Breeders' Cup

events, with a staggering 18 victories, his last coming recently with Saint Liam in the Breeders' Cup Classic in 2005.

As a son of the 1950 Melbourne Cup-winning trainer Jim Cummings, James Bartholomew Cummings knew at an early age where his future lay. Once qualified as a trainer, Cummings proved his versatility by not only winning the long-distance Melbourne Cup, but also sprints such as the major Golden Slipper Stakes for juveniles that he landed on four occasions. He also trained the winner of the prestigious Newmarket Handicap over six furlongs for older horses a record breaking eight times.

His outstanding record in Group One races in Australia included 29 Derby successes, 23 Oaks, six Caulfield Cups, and three Cox Plates. He also holds the record for most Group One winners in a season with 20 victories, and his total Group One triumphs stands at a colossal 245.

But the one shining record, which may never be matched, is his 11 Melbourne Cup successes with ten horses from 1965-99. Think Big was a dual winner in 1974-75.

Cummings has continued to smash records in Australia, receiving numerous awards for his achievements, and was given the opportunity of carrying the Olympic torch at his favourite racetrack, Flemington, in 2000.

Andre Fabre, the son of a diplomat and a law graduate, is one of the most respected trainers around, having sent out winners all across the globe. After a successful career as a jump jockey with over 250 winners, he turned his hand to training, first in the National Hunt arena, before moving onto the Flat. It was on the Flat that Fabre excelled, winning every major French race including the Arc six times. Among his overseas achievements were winning the Canadian International, Dubai Sheema Classic, two Irish Derbies, four English Classics, along with four Breeders' Cups.

Left
French Trainer Andre Fabre at Deauville Racecourse, 2000.

He is without doubt one of the top three European Flat trainers of all-time, and has taken the Champion trainer's title in France on a remarkable 19 successive occasions since 1987.

As an indication of the changing face of racing, former policeman, Saeed Bin Suroor took out his first training licence in 1994. The following year he took over as the main trainer for the Godolphin outfit and divides his time between the Al Quoz stables in Dubai and Moulton Paddocks in Newmarket. Bin Suroor has been Champion trainer three times and has won each Classic at least once, along with three Arcs.

Below
Saeed bin Suroor (left) collects the trophy for the Godolphin stable after winning the Cathay Pacific Hong Kong Mile with Firebreak during the Cathay Pacific Hong Kong International, 2004.

CHAPTER 5
OWNING

Many racing enthusiasts have a dream that, one day, they will own a horse. To be in the paddock before a race, stroking the horse, before wishing the jockey good luck, and listening to the trainer giving final instructions on how to ride the race.

For some, that dream comes true, but for others it is nothing more than a fantasy. To own a racehorse is not only just an expensive hobby, especially for a sole owner, but also a very risky one, with no guaranteed returns. There can also be a sentimental involvement attached to owning a racehorse that may one day be brought to a premature end on the racecourse or gallops. However, in order to experience the ultimate, the owner must be willing to pay the ultimate price, if they are to participate fully in the 'sport of kings'.

Any individual can purchase a racehorse at the sales for as little as they would pay for a car, with the basement being around a thousand pounds. But the very best thoroughbreds trade in the million pound plus bracket, with annual training fees, anywhere from £10,000 upwards; the best trainers charge the highest fees.

However, a new form of owning racehorses has emerged in recent years that enables everyone to have at least a share in a horse with the advent of the racing syndicate. These syndicates, or racing clubs have spread rapidly over the past few decades, making it relatively economical for the average racing enthusiast to become involved in owning a horse. These racing clubs offer shares which cover all the training and entry costs, and can be purchased from as little as a £50 annual fee to £250 for a one per cent interest. Then, for the wealthy, there are the bigger shares with the more prestigious organisations such as the Royal Ascot Racing Club. This 230-strong syndicate were rewarded for their £6,000 joining fee, and £4,700 annual subscription, when greeting home the Derby winner, Motivator, in 2005. The sight of a packed Epsom winner's enclosure that year further promoted the involvement of racing clubs, and they are a welcome source of finance to the horse racing industry.

Below
HM the Queen Mother at Sandown Park, unveiling a life-size bronze statue of the horse Special Cargo, 2001.

Left
HM Queen Elizabeth II and Prince Phillip enjoy the crowds at Royal Ascot.

Owners in Great Britain also have the choice of joining the ROA – Racehorse Owners Association – whose aim it is to help protect racehorse owners. This organisation promotes the interests of owners, as well as contributing towards the improvement in the financial structure of British racing.

It was all very different for the first known owners of the thoroughbred back in the 18th century, when registering their colours at the Jockey Club in 1762. Amongst this first crop of owners were earls, dukes, a viscount, a lord, and a marquis, who had interests in breeding and owned their own studs.

Two of the earliest successful owners were Bob Sievier, and Jim Joel in the early 1900s. The former owned and trained the great Sceptre, while the latter managed to land 11 Classics until his death in 1940. Since then, there have been a number of popular and well-known owners to come along o light up the horseracing world, including the following horse-lovers.

HM THE QUEEN

Following in the footsteps of her mother, Queen Elizabeth II has maintained a tradition by establishing herself as one of the leading owners in Great Britain.

Although, not as successful as King Edward VII who was the only reigning monarch to win a Derby in 1909, the Queen

has had her fair share of winners, including Dunfermline's victory in the 1977 Oaks and St. Leger. The Queen has also won the leading owners title, and her continued passion for horse racing contributes towards the public's interest in the sport of kings.

ROBERT SANGSTER

The late Robert Sangster owned racehorses from the 1960s, before becoming one of the leading racing figures in the world, with thoroughbreds in England, Ireland, France, United States of America, and Australia.

In the 1970s, he employed the very best in the business, forming a strong team with trainer Vincent O'Brien and jockey Lester Piggott that found success in the Derby and Arc de Triomphe.

Sangster also owned the 1984 Eclipse winner Sadler's Wells, who went on to become a leading sire during the next few decades. He then took the ownership of horses to a professional level by investing huge sums of money in stallions as part of his Coolmore breeding operation. This organisation is now under the control of Sangster's son-in-law John Magnier and partner Michael Tabor. These two titans of the turf have continued the Coolmore success story at Ballydoyle in Ireland to this day, winning numerous Group One events throughout the world.

Above left
Greg Childs (right) celebrates victory with owner Robert Sangster at the Victoria Derby, Australia, 1999.

Above right
Sheikh Mohammed at the races in 1996.

Far right
Horses run freely at Calumet Farm.

SHEIKH MOHAMMED

Goodwood racecourse in 1977 proved to be a significant venue and date in the history of ownership in Great Britain, as it was where Sheikh Mohammed's first victory in this country was recorded. Along with his two brothers, the Maktoums have dominated Flat racing in Britain over the past 30 years, with Sheikh Mohammed setting up his own operation under the banner of Godolphin. This breeding, training and racing operation has also helped establish Dubai firmly on the horseracing map, and the organisation has recorded in excess of 100 Group One winners across the globe.

CALUMET FARM

Calumet Farm, in Kentucky, United States of America, is one of the longest-standing owner-

OWNING

Above
Daniel Wildenstein pictured in 2001.

breeder organisations in the world of racing. Established in 1924 by William Monroe Wright, the famous red and blue silks enjoyed their first major stakes winner with Hadagal in 1933, before Bull Lea lifted their profile further in 1939.

It was not until the 1940s, however, under the guidance of trainer Ben Jones that their dominance began, with Whirlaway landing the US Triple Crown in 1940. Calumet experienced a further Triple Crown success in later years, as well as adding eight Kentucky Derby victories, and the operation still stands strong today, breeding horses from their historic farm.

DANIEL WILDENSTEIN

The late Daniel Wildenstein made his fortune as an international art dealer, before turning his hand to owning racehorses. He made a major splash during the 1970s in France, becoming leading owner, before taking the same title in Britain by landing several Classics. Wildenstein also triumphed in the Arc de Triomphe four times, with Allez France, All Along, Sagace, and Pentre Celebre, while all the time expanding his breeding empire.

After his death in 2001, his son Alec took control of racing matters, and the name Wildenstein continues to send out big-race winners, lifting the Gold Cup at Royal York with Westerner in 2005.

HH AGA KHAN

The famous green and red silks of the Aga Khan were first seen at the racetrack in 1922, only two years before he became the leading owner in both England and France. The success continued over the years with numerous Classic victories on both sides of the English Channel, including five Epsom Derby triumphs.

Since 1960, the current Aga Khan IV has continued the strong family traditions associated with horse racing, purchasing a huge stock of horses from Mme. Dupre along with Marcel Boussac's stable and stud worth almost £5 million during the 1970s. Big-race victories then followed, with the world-famous Shergar landing the Epsom Derby in 1981. The operation is still successful, with Azamour winning the King George VI And Queen Elizabeth Diamond Stakes in 2005.

Left
The Aga Khan III, racehorse owner, leads in Blenheim after winning a Derby race, 1930.

Right
L'Escargot winner of the Grand National in 1975.

Right inset top
Golden Miller clears a fence, 1934.

Right inset below
Arkle at Sandown, 1965.

CHAPTER 6
GREAT HORSES

It is difficult to determine what makes one horse greater than another. Career achievements represent one measure of greatness, while another is the amount of prize money accumulated. A horse's greatness can be judged by the length of time it remained unbeaten, or on a single devastating performance, never to be repeated.

Ask a trainer what makes a great horse, and the reply may well be "class and versatility". In other words, the ability to handle every condition thrown at it, and still come out as a Champion. Such a horse should display enough speed to quicken over a short distance, but also retain stamina for the long haul. It must demonstrate the ability to handle the mud, but also be able to float across a hard dry surface. It must be able to cope with many different terrains, from a stiff hill to the rolling landscape of an undulating track. Most of all, it must possess class.

An individual animal possessing that class can perform under pressure with a balanced temperament. It cannot be taught. Bjorn Borg had class, as did David Gower and Bobby Moore, and so did the great thoroughbreds that have graced racing's history.

NATIONAL HUNT

GOLDEN MILLER – foaled in 1927

Golden Miller, along with Arkle, was one of the greatest steeplechasers of all-time.

Bred in Ireland, 'The Miller' was sent to Cambridge in England after being bought for 500 guineas, where Basil Briscoe, who named him after his parents – Goldcourt and Miller – trained him, and Dorothy Paget owned him.

Aged five, he began his march towards legendary status by taking his first Cheltenham Gold Cup in 1932, after only four runs over fences. He defended the crown successfully the following year, before his only failure at a fence in the Grand National the following month. It was thought, after the race, that Golden Miller was just not a National horse.

Despite the doubters, he was entered for the Grand National again in 1934, after recording a hat-trick of Gold Cups. This was to be his year, though, as he became the first horse in history to record the amazing feat of the Cheltenham Gold Cup and Grand National double.

He was never to win the Grand National again, despite another three attempts, but did add another Gold Cup, to establish a record that may never be broken.

Major victories

1932 Cheltenham Gold Cup
1933 Cheltenham Gold Cup
1934 Cheltenham Gold Cup, Grand National
1935 Cheltenham Gold Cup
1936 Cheltenham Gold Cup

ARKLE – foaled in 1957

Arkle is known to many in the world of horse racing as one of the greatest steeplechasers ever. Purchased by Anne, Duchess of Westminster for 1,1250 guineas as a three-year-old, and named after a mountain located near her house in Scotland, this great horse was trained by Tom Dreaper in Ireland.

In 1962, he made a winning debut in Britain at Cheltenham and later that season finished third in his first Cheltenham Gold Cup behind Mill House. However, he was to enact his revenge in the same race a year later, when defeating Mill House to take the Gold Cup by an impressive five lengths. Arkle was to defend the title for the next two years, whilst taking his second Hennessy Gold Cup, a King George VI Chase and a Whitbread Gold Cup.

Arkle became the undisputed Champion chaser of the 1960s, before his career came to an end during the King George VI Chase at Kempton on Boxing Day 1966 when he broke a pedal bone. Unfortunately, the injury was beyond repair and he was retired to the Duchess's farm in County Kildare in 1969.

The manner in which he met his fences and the accuracy displayed enabled him to go through his entire career without ever falling. He raced under National Hunt Rules 34 times, winning on 26 occasions. The racing public had to wait another 38 years before another horse came anywhere near close to matching his ability, when Best Mate won his third Cheltenham Gold Cup in 2004.

Major victories

1964 Leopardstown Chase, Cheltenham Gold Cup, Irish Grand National, Hennessy Gold Cup
1965 Leopardstown Chase, Cheltenham Gold Cup, Whitbread Gold Cup, Hennessy Gold Cup, King George VI Chase
1966 Leopardstown Chase, Cheltenham Gold Cup

L'ESCARGOT – foaled in 1963

This chestnut gelding certainly lived up to his name (The Snail in French), as he took his time in winning the Grand National. But he achieved widespread recognition for doing so, and in the process granted his owner, Raymond Guest, his long-time dream of winning the Aintree marathon.

It took just 11 months for L'Escargot to work his way up the steeplechasing ladder, including a successful raid to

RACE CARDS
credit

NEWS OF THE WORLD
GRAND NATIONAL 1977

Left
Red Rum is led to the winners enclosure after winning the Grand National, 1977.

America, before his first major test in the 1970 Cheltenham Gold Cup. But he passed with flying colours to the surprise of the punters, having returned at 33-1, and showed it was no fluke by returning to defend his crown the following year.

He finished only fourth in the 1972 Gold Cup, before making his debut in the Grand National. However, his challenge finished at the third fence on that occasion, before improving on that effort by finishing third to Red Rum in 1974.

He went one better the following year, finishing runner-up to Red Rum again, but age was catching up with him, and time was running out.

The following year, aged 12, he was dropped in the weights for the 1975 Grand National, and that helped him to finally get his nose in front of Red Rum's, and at the same time enabling him to become the first horse since Golden Miller to win the Gold Cup and Grand National.

L'Escargot was to come out of retirement for just one more race, as a gallant runner-up in the Kerry National, before joining his owner in America, until his passing in 1985.

Major victories
1970 Cheltenham Gold Cup
1971 Cheltenham Gold Cup
1975 Grand National

RED RUM – foaled in 1965

Red Rum is still one of the most, if not the most, famous racehorse of all-time in Britain. The story of how he rose to such heights smacks of fantasy, became reality.

After a mixed early career as an average performer on both the Flat and over fences, this bay gelding headed to the sales in 1972 under a cloud of injuries. He was purchased by former cab-driver and trainer 'Ginger' McCain on behalf of owner and racing enthusiast Noel Le Mare, once one of Ginger's regulars in the back of his cab.

The trainer sorted out eight-year-old Red Rum's injury problems by walking him in the sea, and guided him to the first of his Grand National victories at Aintree in 1973. He returned the following year to become the first horse to defend his title, and in the process becoming the first winner for 38 years to carry 12 stone.

He was a gallant runner-up on his next two attempts in the Grand National, where he had the burdensome task of giving too much weight away to L'Escargot and Rag Trade in 1975 and 1976 respectively. But 'Rummy', as he became known, was not done for just yet. He returned in 1977, aged 12, and once again carrying 12 stone, to record what has gone down as one of the most amazing performances of all time. He destroyed the other runners that day to come clear by a huge 25 lengths, becoming the first horse for 140 years to win the Grand National three times.

Such was his popularity that he regularly appeared in the media, opening supermarkets and betting shops, until 1995 when he died aged 30 and was buried at his favourite place,

Right
Sea Pigeon (left) ridden by Jonjo O'Neill in 1979.

Right inset
Dawn Run also ridden by Jonjo O'Neill at the Cheltenham Gold Cup, 1986.

the winning post at Aintree, where there is also a life-sized bronze statue of him.

Major victories and achievements

1973 Grand National winner
1974 Grand National winner, Scottish Grand National winner
1975 Grand National runner-up
1976 Grand National runner-up
1977 Grand National winner

SEA PIGEON – foaled in 1970

Not many horses have the versatility to run in the Derby on the Flat, before going on to win a Champion Hurdle. That is what made Sea Pigeon special.

Owner Pat Muldoon sent this bay gelding to trainer Peter Easterby in 1976, hoping that he was somebody who could get the best out of the horse. The move resulted in him finishing fourth in the 1977 Champion Hurdle at Cheltenham. He then took the Scottish Champion Hurdle, before switching back to the Flat, to win the valuable Chester Cup.

The same two races were won again the following year, as well as edging closer in the Champion Hurdle, finishing runner-up, a position he was to fill again in 1979. After another successful switch back to the Flat during the summer of 1979, where he took the prestigious Ebor Handicap at York under top-weight of ten stone, he was lined up for his fourth attempt in the Champion Hurdle in 1980.

Now aged ten, and armed with different tactics on this occasion – patiently waiting at the back of the field – he powered through late to win by seven lengths. The same policy was adopted for his defence in 1981, where he displayed a memorable change of gear to mark himself down as one of the greatest dual-purpose horses the sport has seen.

He was eventually retired in 1982 after accumulating a staggering 37 victories in both racing codes, and lived until he was aged 30 in 2000.

Major victories

FLAT
1977 Chester Cup
1978 Chester Cup
1979 Ebor Handicap

NATIONAL HUNT
1977 Scottish Champion Hurdle
1978 Scottish Champion Hurdle, Fighting Fifth Hurdle
1980 Champion Hurdle, Fighting Fifth Hurdle
1981 Champion Hurdle

DAWN RUN – foaled in 1978

This mare cemented a place in history during 1986, when she became the first horse ever to complete the Champion Hurdle and Cheltenham Gold Cup double.

Trained in Ireland by Paddy Mullins, and owned by Charmian Hill, who also rode her in the early days, this gutsy

14

Left
Desert Orchid winner of the Cheltenham Gold Cup in 1989.

mare carried the support of the Irish in 1984 when scrambling home by less than a length to win the Champion Hurdle under pilot Jonjo O'Neill. The goal after that triumph was to go for the Gold Cup the following year, but injury disrupted her career, and plans were put on hold, as she did not race for another 13 months.

But her reappearance at Punchestown in December 1985 was worth waiting for, as she won impressively by eight lengths – her second success over fences – and the plan for the Gold Cup was back on course. Re-united with Jonjo O'Neill for the big day at Cheltenham, the pair combined after the last to get up for a dramatic victory to trigger some of the biggest celebrations ever witnessed on a British racetrack.

Tragically, though, her career came to a premature end only three months later back over hurdles in France and minus Jonjo O'Neill in the saddle. Nevertheless, she will go down as one of the best mares in National Hunt history.

Major victories

1984 Irish Champion Hurdle, Champion Hurdle
1986 Cheltenham Gold Cup

DESERT ORCHID – foaled in 1979

This likeable grey became a firm favourite with the public during the 1980s and early 90s. There were two main reasons for this. Firstly, as a grey, he stood out like a shining beacon, even more so as he always set off in front. And secondly, he was very courageous, never knowing when he was beaten.

Owned and bred by the Burridge family, and trained by David Elsworth in Britain, this gelding was to first make an impact in 1984 by taking the Tolworth and Kingwell Hurdles. However, it was not until 1986 that he really arrived by landing his first King George VI Chase at Kempton, a race he was to make his own in the coming years.

His crowning glory, however, came in 1989 when he remained unbeaten for almost a year by winning seven consecutive races leading up to The Cheltenham Gold Cup. He did not let down his thousands of supporters that day in March, when he galloped bravely through the testing mud to take racing's Championship event by one-and-a-half-lengths.

Despite only managing to finish third in the same race for the next two years, he won the King George VI Chase twice again, making it a record four in total. It was in the same race in 1991, when Desert Orchid was attempting a fifth victory, that he bowed out after falling three from home. However, it was immediately after this fall that he once again displayed the attributes that had made him one of racing's all-time favourites. Rising to his feet, he raced riderless to the line in front of his adoring fans in the grandstand.

'Dessie' has been paraded regularly at major races since his retirement, and was relocated back to Newmarket with David Elsworth in March 2006, aged 27.

Major victories

1984 Tolworth Hurdle, Kingwell Hurdle

Right
Henrietta Knight, (left) the trainer of Best Mate together with her partner Terry Biddlecombe lead the horse and Jockey Jim Culloty to the enclosure, after winning the Cheltenham Gold Cup, 2004.

Right inset
Eclipse after winning the Derby in 1781.

1986 King George VI Chase
1988 Whitbread Gold Cup, Tingle Creek Chase, King George VI Chase
1989 Cheltenham Gold Cup, King George VI Chase
1990 Irish Grand National, King George VI Chase

BEST MATE – foaled in 1995

Not since Desert Orchid had a horse captured the public's imagination to the same extent, but Best Mate managed to do so at the start of the 21st century.

Part of this was due to the connections of the horse, who were always open about him with the public and willing to share their star. This gelding raced in the colours of owner Jim Lewis' favourite football team, Aston Villa, and was trained by the likeable wife/husband team, Henrietta Knight and Terry Biddlecombe.

But it was on the racetrack that Best Mate earned his popularity medals, consistently treating racing fans to his exceptional skills and the art of jumping a fence with finesse at incredible speed.

After winning seven of his 12 starts under National Hunt Rules, he defied the doubters who questioned whether he would have the stamina for three miles and two furlongs by taking his first Cheltenham Gold Cup in 2002. He went one better at Kempton at the end of 2002 by taking the King George VI Chase in gutsy fashion, before defending his crown at Cheltenham in 2003. In doing so, he became the first horse to win successive Gold Cups since L'Escargot, 32 years previously, and the manner of his impressive display that day, pushed him further into the spotlight.

The following year saw him go off at odds-on when landing the first hat-trick of Cheltenham Gold Cups since the mighty Arkle's achievement in 1966. He never had the chance to record a fourth victory in the race, as injury intervened, and he was only to race a further three times, with the final appearance bringing about his sad death at Exeter racetrack in November 2005. His ashes were scattered behind the winning post at Cheltenham, where a life-sized statue was unveiled at the 2006 Festival. There have only been a few chosen horses to make the headlines in the way the classy Best Mate did.

Major victories
2002 Cheltenham Gold Cup, King George VI Chase
2003 Cheltenham Gold Cup
2004 Cheltenham Gold Cup

FLAT

ECLIPSE – foaled in 1764

This grandson of the Darley Arabian, one of the three original sires that gave birth to the thoroughbred racehorse, was himself one of the first great racehorses.

Named after a total eclipse of the sun, occurring as he was foaled, and bred by the Duke of Cumberland, he was owned firstly by William Wildman and then Dennis O'Kelly.

ALSTONS

This chestnut colt never actually saw the racetrack until he was five-years-old, but he soon made up for lost time. In 1769, Eclipse won all of his nine races, including several King's Plates and the City Silver Bowl, before producing more of the same in 1770, when he won even more King's Plates, sometimes running within days of finishing his last race.

It was no fault of his that Eclipse was never truly tested in the most valuable races, as his owner was not a member of the Jockey Club that granted entry to such races. However, the manner in which he conceded lumps of weight without coming off the bridle, suggested he would have succeeded in the more elevated sphere.

He was a huge success at stud, and the fact that up to 80% of modern racehorses include Eclipse in the bloodlines speaks volumes for his class. He also sired three of the first five winners of the Derby, before sadly passing away in 1789 suffering from colic. His memory lives on, though, as the Eclipse Stakes is run every year at Sandown, and his skeleton is on exhibition in Newmarket.

Major victories

1769 Ascot King's Plate, Canterbury King's Plate, Lewes King's Plate, Lichfield King's Plate, City Silver Bowl

1770 Newmarket King's Plate, Guildford King's Plate, Lincoln King's Plate

TOUCHSTONE – foaled in 1831

This well-built colt, owned and bred by the first Marquess Of Westminster and trained by John Scott, raced during a period that was notable for some quality colts in 1834, and made his mark by taking the St. Leger of that year.

As a four-year-old, he won the Doncaster Cup, a feat he was to repeat as a five-year-old, as well as taking the Ascot Gold Cup in 1836. He was to defend the Gold Cup the following year, before retiring to stud.

A bigger success off the racecourse than on it, he sired over three hundred winners, including several Derby winners, before passing away at the age of 31.

Major victories

1834 St. Leger

1835 Doncaster Cup, Ascot Gold Cup

GLADIATEUR – foaled in 1862

This big bay managed to overcome leg injuries throughout his career to enter the history books, becoming the first French-bred horse to win the English Triple Crown in 1865.

Owned and bred by Count Frederic de Lagrange, and trained by Tom Jennings at Newmarket, this colt did not appear on the racetrack until October in his juvenile year, winning two of his three races; the defeat was due to him being sick at the time.

Despite not being fully fit on his reappearance in 1865, this time owing to lameness, he managed to win the Two Thousand Guineas before going on to take the Derby at Epsom in emphatic fashion. It showed what he could achieve when he had an injury-free preparation. He returned to his homeland to please the thousands of fans who turned up at Longchamp to watch him win the Grand Prix de Paris.

After making a winning return to England at Goodwood, he suffered lameness again, before taking his place in the final leg of the Triple Crown. His defeat of an Oaks winner in the St. Leger was again testament to this 'gladiator', as he could barely canter the week before, and amazingly followed-up just two days later in the Doncaster Stakes.

He won two of his three races later that season, before going unbeaten throughout his four-year-old-career. He again suffered with lameness throughout 1866, with the highlight coming in the Ascot Gold Cup, where he defied rock hard ground to win by a breath-taking 40 lengths. He was retired at the end of that season, and had an average career at stud, until his death in 1876.

Gladiateur put French breeding on the map, and is commemorated by a statue at the Longchamp racetrack.

Major victories

1865 Two Thousand Guineas, Derby, St. Leger, Grand Prix de Paris

1866 Ascot Gold Cup, Grand Prix de l'Empereur

ORMONDE – foaled in 1883

Some judge a horse's greatness by how many races it won, or rather how many races it never lost, and not many thoroughbreds retire unbeaten. Ormonde, however, could boast just that and, on his impressive record, he was possibly the best horse of the 19th century.

After a troubled start to his juvenile career due to an injury below the knee, he soon made up the lost time for his owner, the first Duke Of Westminster, when winning all three of his races towards the end of the 1885 season. This John Porter-trained colt reappeared the following season in the Two Thousand Guineas, where he won by two lengths, before winning the Epsom Derby, taking care of The Bard, who was unbeaten in 16 runs and only lost once more after this race.

Ormonde was on course for the Triple Crown, but first managed to win both the St James's Palace Stakes and the Hardwicke Stakes at Royal Ascot within 24 hours of each other. He then took the St. Leger easily by four lengths, before adding a further four victories later that season. However, he was to have a less productive season as a four-year-old, although he did win all three of his races, including two more at Royal Ascot, and the Imperial Gold Cup at Newmarket.

He was then retired as a stallion in 1888, but was less successful than on the racetrack, which may have been due to him being ill at stud, before his passing in 1904.

Major victories

1886 Two Thousand Guineas, Derby, St James's Palace Stakes, Hardwicke Stakes, St. Leger, Champion Stakes

1887 Hardwicke Stakes, Imperial Gold Cup

Left
Fred Archer on Ormonde, 1886. In that year they won the Epsom Derby and the St. Leger Stakes.

Right
Persimmon, winner of the 1899 Derby and the property of King Edward VII, the then Prince of Wales.

Right inset
Isinglass, winner of the Derby and St. Leger in 1893.

ISINGLASS – foaled in 1890

Owned by James Machell, and trained by James Jewitt, Isinglass went into the history books after sweeping all of the top races in England, and in the process accumulating a pot of prize-money that was not to be passed for 60 years.

Isinglass won his first two races as a juvenile, before trumping his main rivals for the following year's Classics in the Middle Park Stakes. He confirmed that form when taking the Two Thousand Guineas at Newmarket in the spring of 1893, despite not being at full fitness, before showing the signs of a true Champion in the Derby, as he was able to win despite not being suited to the bone hard ground.

The final leg of the Triple Crown – the St. Leger at Doncaster – turned out to be a formality, as he won an uncompetitive renewal, before suffering his only career defeat two weeks later.

Switched back to a mile in the Great Lancashire Stakes at Manchester, Isinglass was unable to match the winner for speed and went down admirably by just one length before drawing stumps for the season. He won the Princess Of Wales's Stakes at Newmarket's July meeting on his belated reappearance the following year – the firm surface delaying him – before going on to show his true potential in the Eclipse at Sandown on rain-softened ground.

His only race as a five-year-old was also to be his last, winning the Ascot Gold Cup in 1895 prior to retiring, having won 11 of his 12 races, an amazing achievement as the majority of them came on unsuitably firm ground.

Major victories

1892 Middle Park Stakes
1893 Two Thousand Guineas, Derby, St. Leger
1894 Princess Of Wales's Stakes, Eclipse Stakes, Jockey Club Stakes
1895 Ascot Gold Cup

PERSIMMON – foaled in 1896

This lengthy Royal colt, bred and owned by the Prince of Wales, and trained by Richard Marsh, made a very favourable first impression by taking the Coventry Stakes at Royal Ascot in 1898.

He finished that first season having won two of his three races while his only defeat was due to coughing before the Middle Park Stakes won by St Frusquin – he was rested ahead of his three-year-old campaign. After being slow to come to hand at the start of the Flat season, he bypassed the Two Thousand Guineas – won by a horse that was becoming something of an arch-enemy, St Frusquin, and went straight for the Epsom Derby, where he took on the Newmarket winner.

Persimmon rewarded his connections' patience by landing the Derby, but was to be defeated by St Frusquin at Royal Ascot. Unfortunately, there was to be no further clash between the pair, as the Guineas winner was injured, which left Persimmon a simple task in scooping the St. Leger at long

PERSIMMON

Left
The racehorse Sceptre, 1911.

odds-on. The son of the great St Simon signed off for the season by adding the Jockey Club Stakes, which was worth more prize-money then than either the Derby or St. Leger.

Persimmon became an even better racehorse at four, as he had finally filled his frame, and looked the ultimate thoroughbred. He was then in his prime and on his reappearance, put up his career-best effort in taking the Ascot Gold Cup over two-and-a-half miles by a huge eight lengths. He then marked himself down as a great horse by stepping back in distance to use his speed in taking the Eclipse at Sandown on his final run. It would be unheard of to attempt such a feat these days.

However, those two winning runs came on firm ground that dry year, resulting in injuries to both feet and he was retired as a stallion to the Royal Stud at Sandringham.

He was just as successful at stud, where he produced four Classic winners, including the great Sceptre, before passing prematurely aged 15 due to a broken pelvis.

Major victories

1898 Coventry Stakes, Richmond Stakes
1899 Derby, St. Leger, Jockey Club Stakes
1900 Gold Cup, Eclipse Stakes

SCEPTRE – foaled in 1899

To enter any list of 'greats' requires a great achievement, and this tough as teak mare performed one in 1902.

Bought by Bob Siever in 1900 for a then record 10,000 guineas, she had several trainers including her owner, and raced three times as a juvenile before her big year. That season was to get underway with her finishing a close runner-up in the Lincoln Handicap, before being sent on mission impossible: to win both Guineas races at Newmarket. After taking the first, the Two Thousand Guineas, in a record time, she had only 48 hours to recover before the One Thousand Guineas. But such was her toughness, that she took the race with ease.

The same tactics were applied at Epsom, in an attempt to win both the Derby and Oaks, but she missed out on the former, finishing fourth due to a poor ride, before reappearing two days later to take the latter race.

This pattern was repeated at Royal Ascot, when she was given a bad ride in the Coronation Stakes, before predictably taking the St James's Palace Stakes 24 hours later. It was Glorious Goodwood next, and once again, she failed in her first race, the Sussex Stakes, before running herself fit to land the Nassau Stakes later in the week. However, this pattern suffered a reversal at Doncaster, when she won the St. Leger on her first run of the week, before getting beaten in the Park Hill Stakes two days later.

She changed hands for the following season, but carried on her winning spree, taking in the Hardwicke Stakes, Jockey Club Stakes and the Champion Stakes, before her form dipped the following year and she was retired to the paddocks.

Right
Man O'War, 1937.

Right inset top
Australian racehorse Phar Lap, 1929.

Right inset below
Canadian Jockey John 'Red' Pollard holds a microphone up to the mouth of winning race horse Seabiscuit, 1938.

Major victories

1902 One Thousand Guineas, Two Thousand Guineas, Oaks, St James's Palace Stakes, Nassau Stakes, St. Leger

1903 Hardwicke Stakes, Jockey Club Stakes, Duke Of York Stakes, Champion Stakes

MAN O'WAR – foaled in 1917

This big, chestnut colt, trained in America by Louis Feustel, and owned by Samuel Riddle, consistently raised the bar, breaking three course records as well as three world records.

'Big Red', as he was known, had a career that only spanned two seasons, but he achieved much in a short period, finishing his career with an amazing 20 victories from 21 races, and racking up $249,465 in prize-money.

He won all of his first six events, before losing his only race at Saratoga in 1919, due to a slow start when he faced the wrong way at the tape, but still finished a close runner-up behind Upset, a horse he was to defeat in each of their five other clashes.

He made up for that defeat by taking the Preakness and Belmont Stakes later that season, but was never entered in the Kentucky Derby.

Man O'War was able to give lumps of weight away in handicaps, which in the end led to his retirement. After his final victory in the Kenilworth Park Gold Cup in Canada, it was decided that he would not be asked to concede masses of weight the following year, as a four-year-old, as too much lead in the saddle may have caused a fatal injury.

He retired to stud in Kentucky, where he became leading sire in 1926 despite being sent only the owner's mares, and he produced the great War Admiral. He died in 1947, aged 30, and his open casket was honoured in an unprecedented way by some 2,000 fans at his funeral.

Major victories

1920 Preakness Stakes, Belmont Stakes, Kenilworth Park Gold Cup, Jockey Club Stakes.

PHAR LAP – foaled in 1926

This Australian legend lost his first four races, but went on to greatness, resulting in a film being made about his eventful career that included 37 victories from 51 runs, and a run of 14 straight successes.

Owned and trained by Harry Telford, this New Zealand-bred horse not only won most of Australia's top races but also won some of them twice, including the Randwick Plate, Cox Plate, Melbourne Stakes, and King's Plate. He also recorded record times in the AJC Derby and the Victoria Derby, as well as securing the prestige Melbourne Cup, breaking another record in the process to be the first odds-on favourite.

His defeat in the 1931 Melbourne Cup, when not fully fit, was to be the last time his adoring Australian fans would see of him at home. He was sent over to America in 1932 to prove himself in the Aqua Caliente Handicap, America's richest race at the time, and again he put on one of his best displays to win easily in a record time, announcing himself to the world at large.

However, soon after the Americans were introduced to this legend, he was sadly taken from the world of racing, when he mysteriously died of poisoning in California. This could have been due to nearby trees being sprayed with insecticide.

He was the equine representation of the way Australian athletes compete in sports, with plenty of heart, and Phar Lap's large frame contained one of the biggest.

Major victories

1929 AJC Derby, Victoria Derby, AJC St. Leger, AJC Plate, AJC Craven Plate

1930 AJC Randwick Plate, AJC Craven Plate, WS Cox Plate, Melbourne Stakes, VRC King's Plate, Melbourne Cup

1931 AJC Randwick Plate, AJC Craven Plate, WS Cox Plate, Melbourne Stakes, VRC King's Plate

1932 Aqua Caliente Handicap (America)

SEA BISCUIT – foaled in 1933

Sea Biscuit may not have won the biggest races, but not many horses have a film named after them, and that is in itself a sign of greatness.

This gutsy animal made few splashes during his early career, but after being sent by owner George Smith to trainer Tom Smith, he was introduced to rider Red Pollard and rapid improvement soon came about in the shape of a couple of valuable handicaps. But it was towards the end of 1936 that he really started to shine in California, where he won two more major handicaps in fast times.

The start of the following year saw him beaten in better handicaps, such as the valuable Santa Anita Handicap, before making amends in stakes events throughout the rest of the season that produced 11 victories from 15 races during 1937.

1938 was to bring Sea Biscuit a new jockey, George Woolf as Pollard was injured, and the pair went very close to winning the Santa Anita Handicap trying to concede the winner over two stones. However, he was to have his finest hour later that year in November, when the popular Western horse came head-to-head with the Triple-Crown winner War Admiral, who was the hero of the East in a specially arranged match in Pimlico.

Sea Biscuit did not let his thousands of fans down that day, as he led from pillar to post, dishing out a four length beating to War Admiral, then Horse of the Year. Sea Biscuit also broke the track record in that race, which contributed towards him taking over the title as Horse of the Year in 1938.

An injury in the early part of 1939 put paid to the remainder of that season, and it was a year before he returned to the track where he resumed winning ways on his third run back. He was now being aimed at the one race that had eluded him,

2
NBC
NBC

7
7

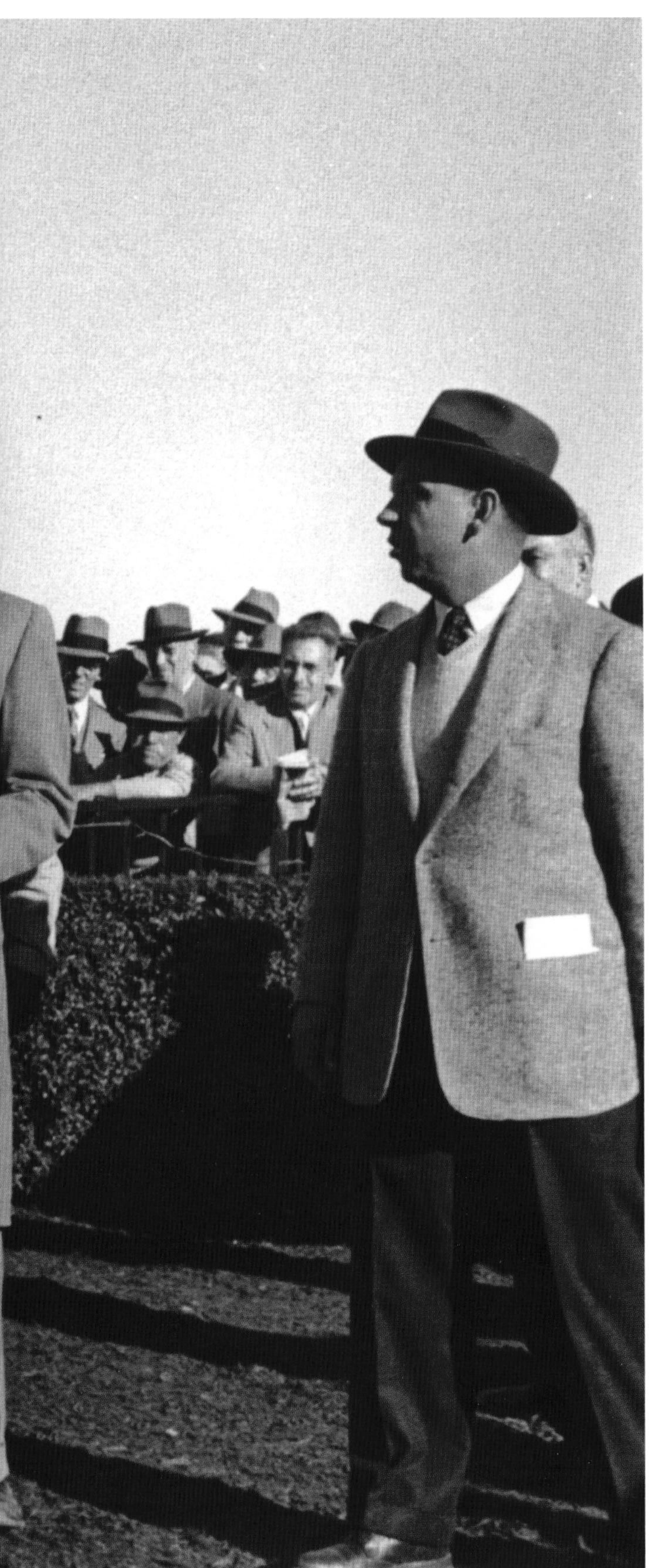

Left
Owner A. G. Vanderbilt with his racehorse Native Dancer after winning the Fall Highweight Handicap at Belmont Park in New York, 1952.

the Santa Anita Handicap worth $121,000, where he was reunited with his old partner Red Pollard, who had himself recovered from injury. Again, he surpassed himself, pulling out all the stops to win by two-and-a-half-lengths to capture the hearts of the thousands watching.

He was retired to stud in California after this triumph, until his premature death at just 14, when the heart that had elevated him to stardom finally gave way.

Major victories

1938 Pimlico Stakes, Hollywood Gold Cup
1940 Santa Anita Handicap

WAR ADMIRAL – foaled in 1934

Known more for his great clash with Sea Biscuit in 1938, War Admiral was himself a great horse.

Owned by Samuel Riddle, and trained by George Conway, this medium-sized brown horse lost as many races as he won as a juvenile, but after strengthening work over the winter returned more muscled in 1937.

He was to take the Triple Crown that season in spectacular fashion, with the Belmont Stakes being won in particularly brave fashion as he tore part of his hoof away when playing up in the starting stalls; it was a habit that plagued his career. After recovering form that injured hoof, he returned just over four months later to win his final three races and scoop the Horse of the Year title.

The following year, War Admiral's 11-race winning run finally came to halt in the Massachusetts Handicap in Boston, in heavy mud, the reason why Sea Biscuit had been taken out of the race, but they finally met on November 1. It was not to be War Admiral's day, however, as Sea Biscuit beat him comprehensively. But he bounced back like a Champion just 11 days later, to land the Rhode Island Handicap and restore his reputation.

He was retired the following year, after suffering an injury to his ankle, but went on to become a leading stallion, before being laid to rest next to his great father Man O'War in 1959.

Major victories

1937 Kentucky Derby, Preakness Stakes, Belmont Stakes
1938 Jockey Club Gold Cup, Saratoga Handicap, Saratoga Cup, Wilson Stakes

NATIVE DANCER – foaled in 1950

This grey – known as 'The Grey Ghost' was one of the greatest thoroughbreds in American history not to have won the Triple Crown.

He was bred and owned by Alfred Vanderbilt and trained by Bill Winfrey, who was responsible for him winning a sensational 21 of his 22 races. Eight of those victories came in his first year as a juvenile in 1952, seven of them in stakes races, to earn him the Horse of the Year title.

He had grown during the winter of 1952/53, and returned to the track as an intimidating individual when landing the

Right
Champion French horse Sea Bird II is led into the enclosure after victory at Epsom in 1965.

Right inset
Ribot, is petted by the owner's daughter, in the winner's enclosure after a race in 1956.

Wood Memorial in preparation for his assault on the Triple Crown. The first-leg, the Kentucky Derby, was to see him suffer his only career defeat, but he stormed through to be a gallant runner-up. He made amends for that defeat by winning the remaining legs of the Triple Crown – the Preakness and Belmont Stakes – in workmanlike fashion, as well as triumphing in another seven races that season.

Native Dancer only appeared three times on the track in 1954, and it was probably his other appearance, on the cover of Time magazine, which caused the biggest headlines that year, such was his popularity.

He was retired to stud, where he was responsible for producing two Kentucky Derby winners to compensate for the race that had evaded him during his racetrack career, before he died prematurely aged 17 in 1967 from colic.

Major victories

1952 The Hopeful, The Futurity
1953 Preakness Stakes, Belmont Stakes, Arlington Classic, American Derby
1954 Metropolitan Handicap

RIBOT – foaled in 1952

The Italian trained Ribot was arguably the greatest Flat horse to arrive on these shores, and he retired unbeaten after 16 races. Nothing could touch him.

Owned by Marchese Mario Incisa della Rochetta, and trained by Ugo Penco, this bay colt never won any of the Italian Classics as he was not entered due to his smallish size at the time. After taking care of all opposition in his homeland, he was given a severe test when entered in the Prix de l'Arc de Triomphe as a three-year-old. But he won the race comprehensively by three lengths, before heading back to Italy to secure the Premio del Jockey Club.

The following year he proved his stamina by taking the Gran Premio di Milano, run over one mile seven furlongs, by a wide margin and then headed to England for the King George VI and Queen Elizabeth Stakes. Again, he showed his class by taking the race easily in heavy ground, and then later that season defended his 'Arc' crown.

By doing so, he became only the fourth horse to ever lift the crown more than once. His success continued off the track at stud in England and America, where he sired two 'Arc' winners, and became Champion sire three times.

Major victories

1954 Gran Criterium
1955 Prix de l'Arc de Triomphe, Premio del Jockey Club
1956 Gran Premio di Milano, King George VI and Queen Elizabeth Stakes, Prix de l'Arc de Triomphe

SEA-BIRD II – foaled in 1962

This chestnut gelding, owned and bred by Jean Ternynck, and trained by Etienne Pollet, was arguably the greatest French Flat horse of all time.

Jockeys
Gate
22

Left
Nijinsky, ridden by Lester Piggott goes clear to win the Derby, 1970.

Left inset
Nijinsky after winning the 1970 Derby.

After two impressive victories from three runs as a juvenile when his only defeat came in the Grand Criterium, he opened up his three-year-old campaign in superb style. Following an easy pipe opener in the Prix Greffuhle, Sea Bird II won the Prix Lupin with authority by six lengths, and then headed to Epsom for the Derby.

He treated racing fans in Britain to a master class that day in 1965, as he never came off the bridle, scooting classily away from his inferior rivals. But, it was his victory later that season, in the Prix de l'Arc de Triomphe at Longchamp, which marked him down as one of the greats. His opposition that day was possibly the strongest ever, as he came up against the French Derby winner, the Irish Derby winner, the American Derby winner, and the Russian Champion. Sea-Bird II took them all apart to score by six lengths to record one of the greatest performances seen.

He was retired to stud in 1967, and died in 1973.

Major victories

1965 Prix Lupin, Derby, Grand Prix de Saint-Cloud, Prix de l'Arc de Triomphe.

NIJINSKY – foaled in 1967

Owner Charles Engelhard paid a Canadian record of $84,000 for this son of Northern Dancer, which turned out to be money very well spent.

Trained in Ireland, under the guidance of Vincent O'Brien, this bay colt won his first four races in that country before coming over to Britain to land the Dewhurst Stakes comfortably, impressing many in the paddock beforehand.

He returned to Britain in 1970 to take the Two Thousand Guineas as the shortest-priced favourite for over 35 years, before heading to Epsom to defeat the highly thought of French horse, Gyr, in the Derby. It was to be the King George VI and Queen Elizabeth Stakes, though, which was to be his acid test, as he took on the older generation, including the previous year's Derby winner, Blakeney. But just as before, he took the field apart with arguably his best ever performance. Lester Piggott, who rode him that day, held the opinion that Nijinsky was the one of the greatest racehorses of the 20th century.

He may have peaked in the 'King George' that day, as he was a sick horse afterwards despite winning the St. Leger at Doncaster to complete the first Triple Crown since 1935, and in the process stretching his unbeaten run to 11. The season caught up with him on his next two races as he had reportedly lost weight and tasted defeat in the Prix de l'Arc de Triomphe and Champion Stakes. He was then rightly retired to stud in America, where he was to enjoy a successful second career, producing three Derby winners, before his death in 1992.

Major victories

1969 Dewhurst Stakes

1970 Two Thousand Guineas, Derby, Irish Derby, King George VI and Queen Elizabeth Stakes, St. Leger.

Right
Geoff Lewis on Mill Reef being led at Epsom after his victory in the 1971 Derby.

BRIGADIER GERARD – foaled in 1968

Trained by the great Major Dick Hern, and owned by John Hislop, this son of Queen's Hussar booked himself a place in history in 1971 by landing one of the best Two Thousand Guineas ever assembled at Newmarket.

Although he went into the race unbeaten, he came up against two other talented horses in the great Mill Reef, and My Swallow. But, after stylishly taking these notable scalps, it was thought Brigadier Gerard would naturally take his place in the Derby. However, his owner did not think he would get the extra half-mile and was therefore aimed at all the major races between a mile and a mile-and-a-quarter, although he did eventually prove his stamina when landing the King George VI and Queen Elizabeth Stakes at Ascot in 1972.

'The Brigadier' finally lost his unbeaten record just three weeks later in the Benson & Hedges Gold Cup at York, going down by three lengths to the 1972 Derby winner, Roberto, and was retired at the end of that season.

He boasted a high-class record of seventeen victories from 18 races, along with breaking the course records over a mile and a mile-and-a-quarter at Ascot.

Major victories

1971 Two Thousand Guineas, St James's Palace Stakes, Sussex Stakes, Goodwood Mile, Queen Elizabeth II Stakes, Champion Stakes

1972 Lockinge Stakes, Prince Of Wales's Stakes, Eclipse Stakes, King George VI and Queen Elizabeth Stakes, Queen Elizabeth II Stakes, Champion Stakes

MILL REEF – foaled in 1968

In the same way Sebastian Coe and Steve Ovett graced the athletics track during the late-seventies, both Mill Reef and Brigadier Gerard emerged at the same time – the early-seventies – to give horse racing fans in Britain the ultimate treat. The American Paul Mellon bred and owned this small colt who was trained in England by Ian Balding, and had a highly successful juvenile campaign. He was defeated only once, in France by a short head to My Swallow, a horse he was to face again in the Two Thousand Guineas the following season.

However, despite the great Brigadier Gerard putting both colts in their place that day, Mill Reef was never to be defeated again. After easily taking the Derby at Epsom by two lengths, he made light work of beating the talented French horse Caro by four lengths in the Eclipse at Sandown. He then went onto land the King George VI and Queen Elizabeth Stakes just as easily, before proving himself to be the best middle-distance horse in Europe by taking the Prix de l'Arc de Triomphe.

A virus hampered his four-year-old career, but he still managed a couple of stunning victories, before sadly breaking down on the gallops during the summer of 1972, which forced his retirement. But, he proved himself just as successful when standing at stud, before passing away in 1986.

Left inset
Jockey Joe Mercer riding Brigadier Gerard to victory in the Queen Elizabeth II stakes at Ascot, 1972.

Left
Secretariat displaying his beauty running freely in a field, 1978.

There will always be comparisons made between Mill Reef and Brigadier Gerard, and to some, the former was rated as the best all-rounder as he also proved himself to be the best in Europe before becoming a leading stallion.

Major victories

1971 Derby, Eclipse Stakes, King George VI and Queen Elizabeth Stakes, Prix de l'Arc de Triomphe

1972 Prix Ganay, Coronation Cup

SECRETARIAT – foaled in 1970

It was his outstanding performance in the 1973 Belmont Stakes that marked this son of Bold Ruler down as one of the greatest horses in American history.

Owned by Penny Tweedy, and trained by Lucien Laurin, this intelligent chestnut colt learned after his first race how to break from the stalls properly, as he was badly hampered on his debut – his only unplaced run. He soon put that experience behind him by winning his next eight races as a juvenile to propel him into the spotlight.

During his build-up to the Triple Crown as a three-year-old, he tasted defeat in the Wood Memorial but once again, was able to put that to one side when landing the first Leg, the Kentucky Derby, by two-and-a-half lengths from Sham, while smashing the race record.

The second leg of the Triple Crown, the Preakness Stakes, once more saw the race record broken, as Secretariat came from last to first to beat Sham by the same margin. Then came the final leg, the Belmont Stakes. This amazing "machine" as the commentator referred to him, destroyed his rivals, including Sham, to win by a staggering 31 lengths and record a new world record. It was a truly great performance.

During the remainder of that season, he won the Arlington Invitational easily, before tasting defeat twice. He had excuses of illness and wrong ground, but made a successful transition over to the turf for his final two races. After breaking the course record at Belmont Park in the Man O'War Stakes, he took the Canadian International Stakes at Woodbine, breaking the record for earnings in the process, with $1, 316, 808 in the bank.

After a successful career at stud, he died in 1989, aged just 19, in Kentucky where he was also laid to rest.

Major victories

1973 Kentucky Derby, Preakness Stakes, Belmont Stakes, Bay Shore Stakes, Gotham Stakes, Arlington Invitational, Man O'War Stakes, Canadian International Stakes.

ALLEGED – foaled in 1974

Trained in Ireland by the masterful Vincent O'Brien, and owned by Sir Robert Sangster, this late-maturing colt was considered to be one of the best horses associated with the successful owner-trainer team. He did not see the racetrack until the end of the 1976 season, as he was gangly and backward, but still managed to win his debut by eight lengths.

Right
Steve Cauthen of the USA on Affirmed, 1990.

Right inset
Dancing Brave at the 1986 Derby.

Given plenty of time to mature in 1977, he announced himself onto the big stage when landing the Great Voltigeur Stakes at York. However, he was to face his only defeat in the St. Leger next time at Doncaster, being narrowly beaten by the Queen's Dunfermline. But, Alleged was to set the record straight in the Prix de l'Arc de Triomphe, where he took up the running after two furlongs to bound clear easily and leave Dunfermline back in fourth place.

He made a winning reappearance in Ireland the following year, but the firm ground he encountered that day was to cause injuries to his knees, and his career was put on hold until the autumn, when the softer ground helped him. After having a superb preparation race for the Arc in the Prix du Prince D'Orange, where he broke the course record, he marched on to defend his Arc crown in emphatic fashion, to become only the third horse since the war to win the race twice.

To come back from injury and win the Arc marked him down as one the greatest, and he retired to stud, having only lost just one of his ten races, the 1977 St. Leger. But he managed to produce a son, Shantou, who took the 1997 version. He retired from stallion duties in 1997, and died aged 26 in 2000.

Major victories

1977 Great Voltigeur Stakes, Prix de l'Arc de Triomphe
1978 Prix de l'Arc de Triomphe

AFFIRMED – foaled in 1975

Owned by Louis and Patrice Wolfson, and trained by Laz Barrera, Affirmed went into the American history books for the courage he displayed in taking the Triple Crown.

As a juvenile in 1977, this son of Exclusive Native first locked horns with another talented youngster called Alydar for what was to be the first of many battles. The pair had already beaten each other once in 1977, but were kept apart until August when they met in the Hopeful Stakes. Affirmed displayed his customary reserves to beat his rival on the line, and it was the same result just two weeks later in the Futurity Stakes.

However, Alydar exacted his revenge during their next encounter, when wet conditions in the Champagne Stakes counted against Affirmed who was kept to the inside of the track. The final meeting that season was to be in the Laurel Futurity, where Affirmed held his old foe by a neck to earn him the award of Best Colt in 1977.

In 1978, both colts were unbeaten during their preparation for the Kentucky Derby, with Affirmed taking the Santa Anita Derby and the Hollywood Derby. The scene was now set for a showdown in Kentucky. Once again it was to be Affirmed who came out on top, getting first run up the straight, and taking his personal score with Alydar to 5-2. Next up was the Preakness Stakes, and Affirmed this time came eyeball to eyeball with his rival in the straight, before once more pulling out extra under pressure. It was the sign of a great Champion, but better was still come.

In the final leg of the Triple Crown, the Belmont Stakes over a mile-and-a-half, Alydar tested Affirmed's stamina and made it a real test before heading him in the straight. But once again, under jockey Steve Cauthen, he found extra to put his nose in front and claim the Triple Crown. The year ended on a losing note, when failing to beat the older Seattle Slew, who had won the Triple Crown in 1977, before getting back on the winning trail in his final year in 1979.

He landed the Hollywood Gold Cup and the Jockey Club Gold Cup that season, before retiring to take up stallion duties. He was to sire many Champions, before his sad death in 2001, aged 26.

Major victories

1977 Hopeful Stakes, Futurity Stakes, Laurel Futurity, Champagne Stakes.
1978 Kentucky Derby, Preakness Stakes, Belmont Stakes, Santa Anita Derby, Hollywood Derby.
1979 Hollywood Gold Cup, Jockey Club Gold Cup, Santa Anita Handicap, Californian Stakes, Woodward Stakes.

DANCING BRAVE – foaled in 1983

This son of Lyphard was different to many of the other greats because his racing career was rather short, lasting barely two seasons. But it was sweet because it took only one year to seduce the many who were fortunate enough to see him.

Trained by Guy Harwood and owned by Khalid Abdullah, this highly talented colt first set foot on the racetrack in 1985, where he won both races as a juvenile. At the start of the 1986 Flat season, he took the Craven Stakes at Newmarket, before returning to win the Two Thousand Guineas in impressive fashion, so next stop was the Derby at Epsom. However, he was to suffer his only defeat in Europe that day, when becoming unbalanced around the course's unique turns, before finishing runner-up. Many thought he was one of the unluckiest ever losers of the Derby.

He was able to put the record straight two runs later when taking the Eclipse and going on to beat the Derby winner, Shahrastani, in the King George VI and Queen Elizabeth Stakes at Ascot. The Prix de l'Arc de Triomphe then loomed as the race that can decide a true Champion, bringing together as it does the cream of European middle-distance performers. 1986 was to be a vintage year. The race contained over ten Group One performers, but Dancing Brave sailed past all of them to lift the European crown in a record time.

Despite losing in America later, he earned an official rating which has yet be passed, marking him down as one of the true greats.

Major victories

1986 Craven Stakes, Two Thousand Guineas, Eclipse Stakes, King George VI and Queen Elizabeth Stakes, Prix de l'Arc de Triomphe

CITY of PORTSMOUTH
THE DERBY
5

lawn stand
Melbourne

Left
Jockey Glen Boss on Makybe Diva wins the Melbourne Cup for the third year in a row, 2005.

MAKYBE DIVA – foaled in 1999

This British-bred mare hit the headlines around the world in 2005 after her exploits in Australia, where she became the first three-times winner of the prestigious Melbourne Gold Cup.

Unwanted at the sales in Britain, she was sent to the Antipodes where she was purchased by businessman Tony Antic, who named her after the first two letters of five employees at his tuna factory – Maureen, Kylie, Belinda, Diana, Vanessa.

She was trained by David Hall, and made her debut aged four when she won no fewer than six races, including the Queen Elizabeth Stakes over a mile-and-a-half at Flemington.

The following year in 2003, saw her beaten six times, mainly over distances short of her best, before she took the Melbourne Cup at her first attempt over two miles, a distance over which she was only beaten once in five runs. She was then beaten five times in 2004, again over shorter distances, before returning to two miles in the valuable Sydney Cup in April, where she scrapped home by just a short-neck.

That performance made her the first mare to complete the Melbourne Cup/Sydney Cup double, before she went on to complete the Melbourne Cup double in November, this time under trainer Len Freedman.

She took care of a quality field that day, including two Caulfield Cup winners and the 2002 Melbourne Cup winner, as well as some quality staying performers from Europe. That made her one of the best long-distance mares of the modern-era.

After two defeats in February 2005, she showed her amazing versatility by winning the Australian Cup over a mile-and-a-quarter – a race she had finished only sixth in the previous year – back at her beloved Flemington. She was in terrific form at this stage in her life, as a seven-year-old, and demonstrated this by taking the BMW Classic over a mile-and-a-half at Rosehill, just seven days after her Australian Cup triumph.

After two unsuccessful attempts in Japan on ground too firm, she was prepared for her record breaking hat-trick attempt in the Melbourne Cup, and bagged another three victories on her way, including the Cox Plate at Moonee Valley. That victory sent her off as favourite for the big day at Flemington in front of 140,000 race goers, and she did not let her supporters down, coming with her customary late burst to enter the history books by one-and-a-half lengths.

She was retired after this race to start a career in the paddocks at Tony Antic's brother's property Flinders, where it is hoped she will succeed in becoming a valuable broodmare.

Major victories

2002 Queen Elizabeth Stakes
2003 Melbourne Cup
2004 Sydney Cup, Melbourne Cup
2005 Australian Cup, BMW Classic, Memsie Stakes, Turnbull Stakes, Cox Plate, Melbourne Cup

Right
A horse clears a fence at Aintree.

CHAPTER 7 GREAT COURSES

Racecourses throughout the world have come a long way since Chester attracted the locals alongside the River Dee, on an open strip of land in 1540. The modern racecourse these days is equipped with state-of-the-art facilities, in tandem with the best sporting arenas in the world, featuring the very best selection of leisure and entertainment activities.

But, when it comes to variety, British race goers are certainly spoilt for choice, with an array of different venues forming a mouth-watering menu to choose from.

This variation represents the heart of the sport, making a day at the races in this country truly unique. Some of the smaller courses offer pure history, where as others glow in a warm local atmosphere, creating an ideal day out for the family.

The actual tracks on which the races take place are also unique, with Newmarket's wide-open, galloping straight, Chester's greyhound-like tight turns, Epsom's severe undulations, and Windsor's figure of eight dimensions.

Racecourses additionally offer the race goer the chance to physically view a horse in the flesh around the paddock area before racing, an experience in which television viewers are unable to participate.

Then there are the prestige venues such as Ascot and Cheltenham which are very commercially-minded, playing host to high rollers and businessmen with their hospitality suites, while the fashion-conscious are well catered for in the trendy members enclosures.

There are now plenty of these prestige racecourses across the globe, standing shoulder to shoulder amongst the greatest, including the likes of Dubai, Santa Anita, Longchamp, Flemington, and Tokyo.

So what separates a great racecourse from a good one? A great racecourse should provide a relaxed, pleasurable experience unmatched anywhere else, such as at Goodwood, Sussex. Anyone attending a race meeting there can be excused for forgetting they are at the races, due to the stunning scenery that surrounds this undulating course. It offers the chance to amble around leisurely, without any hustle or bustle.

But for others, a great racecourse should offer non-stop excitement from the first race to the last, providing a rush of adrenalin that goes with being in amongst the action, and the following great venues all offer their own individual experience.

ENGLAND

AINTREE – Liverpool

NATIONAL HUNT

A left-handed level course featuring two circuits. The Mildmay Course is one-and-a-half miles round and is sharper than the Grand National course, which is two-and-a-quarter miles, the longest in Britain.

Aintree is the home of the most famous steeplechase in the world – the Grand National run over four-and-a-half miles – and provides a window for many into the world of horseracing.

The course first staged racing in 1829, after Lord Sefton leased the land, but it was not for another ten years until the big race was first run in 1839. The inaugural Grand National saw horses jumping jagged hedges, brooks, a stone wall, and paling. The fences that face the runners these days, however, are a lot tamer but are still the stiffest and most feared in Britain, giving Aintree its recognisable character.

The Grand National is not the only big race to be staged at Aintree, as it also plays host to the following major events:

April – **Melling Chase over two-and-a-half miles**

April – **Sefton Novices' Hurdle over three miles**

April – **Maghull Novices' Chase over two miles**

April – **Aintree Hurdle over two-and-a-half miles**

Lord Sefton sold the course to the Topham family in 1949, and they built a new track within the National course, naming it after the amateur jockey Lord Mildmay. 1953 was a big year for the course, as not only did they open the Mildmay Course, but also a motor circuit, which staged the British Grand Prix on several occasions.

Aintree endured some uncertain times during the sixties and seventies – including the final Flat race meeting to be staged there in 1976 – changing

CHAPTER 7

GREAT COURSES

ownership on a few occasions, but it has been on solid ground since the Racecourse Holdings Trust took over.

The famous venue is now looking ahead to a redevelopment plan, which will update the course in time for the 2007 Grand National.

Left
Royal Ascot 2006, with the newly completed £200m grandstand in the background.

ASCOT – Berkshire

FLAT AND NATIONAL HUNT.

A triangular right-handed circuit of over a mile-and-three-quarters, with the home straight three furlongs long, joining the straight mile. All races, which are shorter than a mile, are run on the straight course.

The course is wide and galloping, with a testing run-in that rises before levelling out at the winning post.

One of the most popular racecourses in the world, Ascot hosts the Royal Meeting every year in mid-June. The Royal connection goes back to the days of Queen Anne who first spotted the vacant area of land where Ascot now stands and purchased it for just over £558. It was then decided for a course to be built there, which led to the first meeting getting underway in August 1711. The founder of Ascot has a race named after her, which is run on the first day of the Royal Meeting –the Queen Anne Stakes.

Royal Ascot was first held in 1768 – then over four-days – and is the biggest meeting held during the Flat season, staging no few than six Group One races over five days as follows:

June – St James's Palace Stakes over a mile for three-year-olds

June – Queen Anne Stakes over a mile for four-year-olds and above

June – Prince of Wales's Stakes over a mile-and-a-quarter for three-year-olds and above

June – Gold Cup over two miles-and-a-half for four year olds and above

June – Coronation Stakes over a mile for three-year-old fillies

June – Golden Jubilee Stakes over six furlongs for three-year-olds and above

Ascot is full of tradition. The procession where the Royal carriages enter the racecourse at the start of the straight mile, parading in front of race goers before they take their seats in the Royal Enclosure, has been a feature since 1825. Another tradition, which rings loud during every race at Ascot, is the bell that is heard as the runners enter the home straight – originally used to alert and clear people walking across the course.

There are two other major fixtures that take place on the Flat at Ascot, the 'King George' and 'Festival' meetings, held in July and September. The former three-day meeting features the Group One King George VI and Queen Elizabeth Diamond Stakes over one and-a-half miles for three year-olds and above. This race often brings together the clash of the generations, where the current Derby winner aged three, is tested against his elders. The Ascot Festival over three days features the Group One Queen Elizabeth II Stakes over a mile for three-year-olds and above, and was first run in 1955.

Ascot has staged National Hunt fixtures throughout the winter since 1965, and as with the Flat, it attracts the best horses due to the quality events held. These include Grade One and Two races such as:

December – Long Walk Hurdle over three miles and one furlong
January – Victor Chandler Chase over two miles
February – Ascot Chase over two-and-a-half miles
February – Reynoldstown Novices' Chase over three miles

There was no racing at Ascot during 2005, as the course took a major step into the future, spending £200 million on redevelopment, the largest amount on course regeneration ever seen in Europe. The main improvement is the new grandstand, which will give a much more modern feel to the place when it is re-opened in June 2006, launching Ascot into the future.

CHELTENHAM – Gloucestershire

NATIONAL HUNT.

A left-handed undulating track with a testing uphill finish. There are two separate courses – the Old and New – which are both oval and are a mile-and-a-half long.

Cheltenham is looked upon as the home of National Hunt racing – similar to Newmarket on the Flat – and is ideally located in the Cotswolds, creating the ideal theatre. Racing first took place there in 1815, with the inaugural meeting as such in 1818. The very first Cheltenham Gold Cup was staged a year later, and to the horror of modern National Hunt enthusiasts, it was run over the flat! It wasn't until 1845 that the first steeplechase took place, and then twenty years later, the first proper course was developed.

The Cheltenham Festival, with which it is so proudly associated these days, first took place in 1902 and lasted just two days, in comparison with the four-day affair that was introduced in 2005. Twenty-two years later, the first Cheltenham Gold Cup Steeplechase was held, with the Champion Hurdle following three years later in 1927.

The decision to extend the Festival to three days was made in 1949, and punters from across the Irish Sea were heard aloud as the Gold Cup went to Ireland.

1959 welcomed the first running of the National Hunt Two Mile Champion Chase – later to be known as the Queen Mother Champion Chase.

The racecourse engaged in ongoing developments due to its growing popularity, from the 1960s until the late 1980s, which resulted in new paddocks, stables, restaurants and stands.

The progress has continued at Cheltenham since the Millennium, with more investment resulting in superb facilities, bringing the course into line with the finest in Britain. The four-

Right
Runners head to the first flight during the Cheltenham Annual National Hunt Festival in 2005.

CHESTER
0800 73 11 210

day Festival in March – the jewel in Cheltenham's crown – is now arguably the most popular in the racing calendar. Tickets constantly sell out due to the massive demand from racing enthusiasts wanting to see the jumping Champions crowned in this magnificent arena. The Grade One races, which decide such Champions, are as follows:

March – **Supreme Novices' Hurdle over two miles**
March – **Arkle Trophy over two miles**
March – **Champion Hurdle over two miles**
March – **Royal & Sun Alliance Novices' Hurdle over two miles and five furlongs**
March – **Royal & Sun Alliance Chase over three miles**
March – **Queen Mother Champion Chase over two miles**
March – **Champion Bumper over two miles**
March – **World Hurdle over three miles**
March – **Triumph Hurdle over two miles and one furlong**
March – **Cheltenham Gold Cup over three miles and two furlongs**

Cheltenham racecourse has come a long way in recent years in an attempt to move into the future, but it has not forgotten its heroes of the past. Statues of Champions Golden Miller, Arkle, Dawn Run, and now Best Mate stand proudly as a reminder of what Cheltenham represents: pure class.

CHESTER – Cheshire

FLAT

A left-handed, flat circuit of just over a mile, with very tight turns and a short run–in.

'The Roodee' as it is known, is situated next to the River Dee and first staged racing back in 1540, making it the oldest racecourse in Britain.

It earned its nickname back in Roman times, when part of the River Dee dried up, and the area was marked with a cross – or rood – which still remains on the site.

There is a fascinating history associated with Chester racecourse, with the east side of the circuit surrounded by the Roman walls, and the south side displaying the Grosvenor Bridge, which was used for the Romans' transport.

The course was just a bare field until 1817, when the first grandstand was built. This stand was replaced in 1900 by the County Stand, before it was damaged by fire in 1985, and replaced with more modern facilities – giving it a balance of old and new whilst retaining its heritage. The place also has an intimacy lost at other racecourses, with the paddock on the inside of the circuit alongside the winning line and in front of the stands.

Chester's main attraction each year is the three-day Festival in May, which centres around the competitive Chester Cup, run over two-and-a-quarter miles, founded in 1858. There are also several other significant races that take place at this historic racecourse including the following:

May – **Chester Vase over a mile-and-a-half for three-year-olds**
May – **Dee Stakes over a mile and-a-quarter for three-year-olds**
May – **Ormonde Stakes over a mile and five furlongs**
May – **Cheshire Oaks over one mile three furlongs for three-year-old fillies**
July – **City Wall Stakes over five furlongs**

DONCASTER – South Yorkshire

FLAT AND NATIONAL HUNT

A left-handed, pear-shaped course just short of two miles long, with the only undulation coming in the back straight on Rose Hill. There is also an adjoining straight course over one-mile for flat racing.

Horse racing first took place in Doncaster in the area of Town Moor as far back as 1595, with the Doncaster Cup being born years later in 1766. Ten years after came the first British Classic – the St. Leger, then over two miles – and such was the popularity of horse racing here, that a new grandstand and course was developed.

Doncaster also stages the Lincoln Handicap, which was first run in 1858, before being located to Town Moor from Lincoln racecourse in 1965. This race traditionally triggers the start of the Flat season in late-March, whereas the November Handicap – which was moved here from Manchester in 1964 – signals the close. National Hunt racing takes place here after the Flat season, and hosts the Great Yorkshire Chase over three miles in January.

The main event to take place at Doncaster during the Flat season is the four-day St. Leger meeting in early September, which not only features the historic race itself – now run over one mile six furlongs – but also the following Group races:

September – **Park Hill Stakes over a mile and-a-quarter for fillies and mares**
September – **May Hill Stakes over a mile for two-year-old fillies**
September – **Park Stakes over seven furlongs for three-year-olds and above**
September – **Doncaster Cup over two miles two furlongs for three-year-olds and above**
September – **Champagne Stakes over seven furlongs for two-year-old colts and geldings**
September – **Flying Childers over five furlongs for two-year-olds**

The Group One Racing Post Trophy is also held in October, over a mile for juveniles – a useful pointer towards the following year's Classics.

The last major development to take place at the racecourse was in 1969, when a new grandstand was built, with the parade ring being re-located in front. But in an attempt to move with the times, Doncaster closed its gates at the end of 2005 for further redevelopment. The Yorkshire Stand will be demolished and re-built, along with brand new stables, and a hotel, which will be in place for the 2007 St. Leger.

Left top
The May Festival at Chester, 2006.

Left bottom
The Doncaster Cup, Doncaster.

Right
The Stanley Racing Handicap Stakes at Epsom Racecourse, 2002.

Right inset
The St Pauls Catholic College Banded Stakes run at Kempton Park, 2006.

EPSOM – Surrey

FLAT

A left-handed undulating, horseshoe-shaped track measuring a mile-and-a-half long. It also has an adjoining five-furlong straight for sprint races, as well as separate chutes for the six and seven furlong races.

Epsom Downs stages two of the five English Classics – the Derby and Oaks, both over a mile-and-half – and has staged racing since 1625. The first recorded race meeting took place in 1661, and in 1684, they employed their first clerk of the course. Regular meetings then got underway from 1730, before the introduction of the Oaks in 1779, which was followed a year later by the Derby.

It was not until 1784, however, that the famous bend – Tattenham Corner – leading into the home straight was introduced, and the race was lengthened to a mile-and-a-half. The course used nowadays, has been in place since 1872, where the runners set-off on the opposite side of the stands to race up and down Tattenham Hill, before sweeping into the home bend. The straight sprint course, which joins Tattenham Corner at the home bend, is downhill all the way and is the fastest five furlongs in the world.

Epsom also offers its own unique atmosphere on Derby Day, as the centre of the circuit is used to create a carnival occasion, welcoming open-top buses, as well as staging a funfair and musical concerts. The racecourse has kept up with the changes, redeveloping the grandstands, including the Queen's Stand, opened in 1992.

The two-day Derby meeting in early-June stages another Group One race – the Coronation Cup over a mile-and-a-half for older horses – as well as the following:

June – Princess Elizabeth Stakes over a mile for fillies and mares three-years-old and above

June – Diomed Stakes over a mile for three-year-olds and above

As well as staging such a prestige meeting, Epsom provides race fixtures towards the other end of the scale, featuring the Amateur Derby in August – run since 1960 – while many of the evening meetings attract plenty of commuters from London.

KEMPTON PARK – Middlesex

FLAT (ALL-WEATHER) AND NATIONAL HUNT

A right-handed, level track, with an all-weather circuit and a National Hunt turf course.

Kempton Park was opened in July 1878, after conservative politician Henry Hyde spotted the land for sale during a trip to London. The first major race to take place there was the Jubilee Stakes – founded in 1887 – marking the fiftieth year of the reign of Queen Victoria.

The racecourse suffered a setback in 1932, when fire destroyed the grandstand, restaurant, Member's Stand and Tattersalls bar. But, there were better times ahead for

KEMPTON PARK
14
13
12
11
10

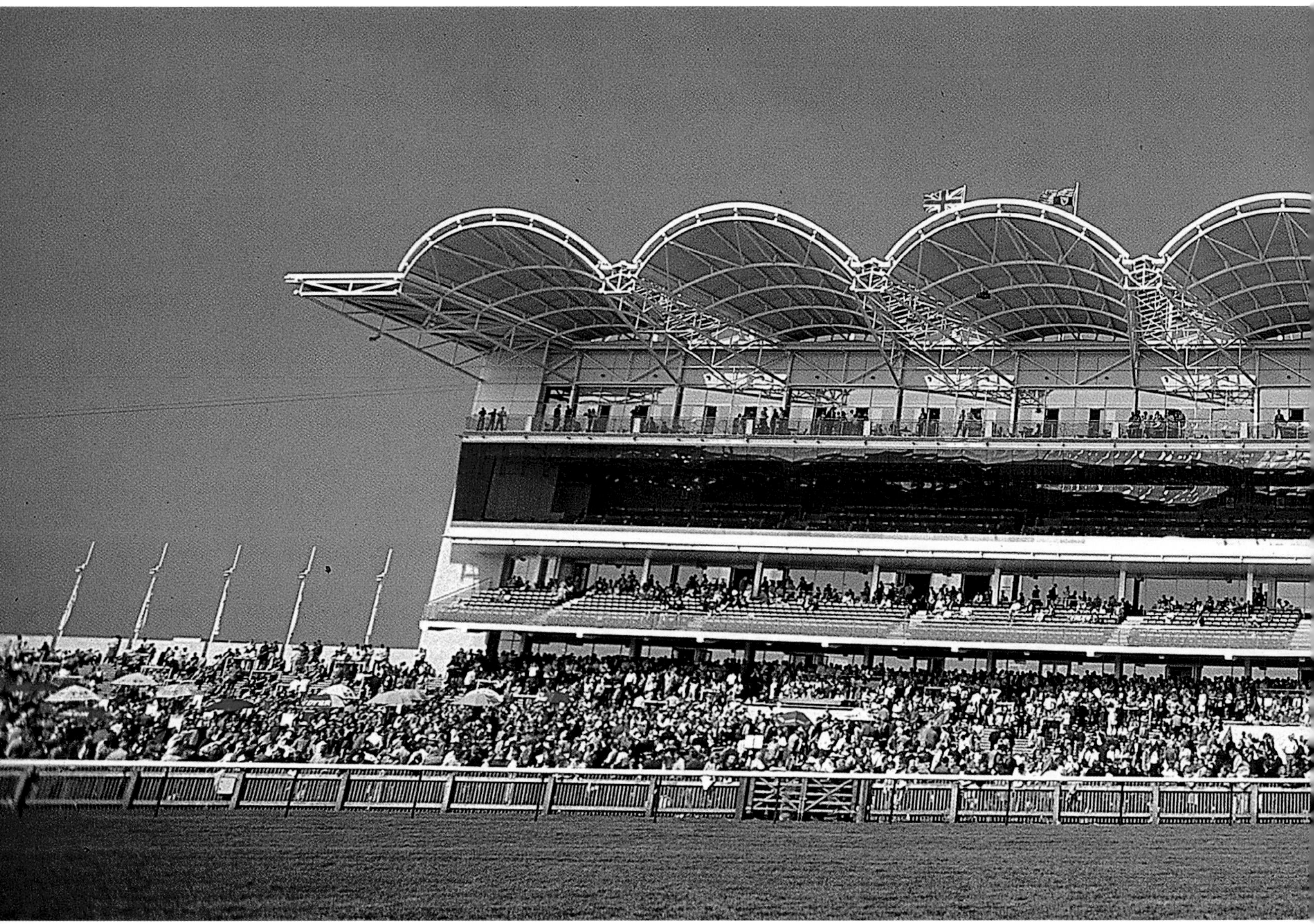

Kempton, when the inaugural running of the King George VI Chase took place in February 1938 – now run every Boxing Day – and despite the participation of just four runners, it was to later become the venue's flag-bearer. Being one of the most popular races in the National Hunt calendar, the racecourse welcomed the television cameras in 1949 to cover the King George.

Such is Kempton's closeness to London – the nearest course to Central London – that crowds grew in the 1950s, with the Easter meeting attracting a record 54,000 people.

In 1972, Kempton staged the first-ever race under Rules for lady riders in Britain, which was also the same period a new clubhouse – with weighing room – was built, and the parade ring re-located. It was not until 1997 that a spanking new grandstand was constructed, featuring a glass-fronted restaurant, which stood above the new parade ring.

One of the most significant changes happened at Kempton in March 2006, when Flat Turf racing was transferred over to an artificial surface, making it the first right-handed all-weather course in Britain. It also installed floodlights, which will attract a new evening audience, but the track has maintained all of its key races from the Flat Turf programme including:

April – **Magnolia Stakes over a mile-and-a-quarter for older horses**

April – **Easter Stakes over a mile for three-year-old colts and geldings**

April – **Queen's Prize over two miles for older horses**

April – **Jubilee Handicap Stakes over a mile for older horses**

The National Hunt fixture-list continues to boast a wealth of top races as well, to accompany the King George VI Chase, including these Grade class events:

Left
The Millennium Grandstand during the Guineas meeting at Newmarket, 2000.

December – Feltham Novices' Chase over three miles
December – Christmas Hurdle over two miles
February – Rendlesham Hurdle over three miles
February – Racing Post Chase over three miles

NEWMARKET - Suffolk

FLAT

July Course – a right-handed, undulating track up to two miles long, with a wide mile-long galloping straight, and an uphill finish.

Rowley Mile – a right-handed, undulating track up to two and-a-quarter miles long, with a wide, nine furlong galloping straight, and an uphill finish.

In 1622, Lord Salisbury and the Marquess of Buckingham ran their horses against each other in a 'match' close to the New Market of Exning, giving birth to horse racing in Newmarket, and its two separate courses. The Rowley Mile is used during the spring and autumn, while the July Course is used during the summer months.

Racing was temporarily put on hold at Newmarket around 1654, several years after Charles I's reign, before King Charles II sparked it back into life, naming one of the courses after his hack 'Old Rowley'.

Racing ticked along at Newmarket for the next hundred years under James II and William of Orange, before the Jockey Club was founded in the area during 1750, which gradually led towards Newmarket being looked upon as the headquarters of horse racing.

The introduction of two of the five English Classics between 1809-14 – the Two Thousand Guineas and One Thousand Guineas – gave Newmarket the big races it deserved, followed in the coming years by these Group One races:

Right
Frankie Dettori and Excellent Art come home to land the wbx.com World Bet Exchange E.B.F. National Stakes run at Sandown Park, 2006.

July – Falmouth Stakes over a mile for fillies and mares
July – July Cup over six furlongs for three-year-olds and above
October – Cheveley Park Stakes over six furlongs for juvenile fillies
October – Middle Park Stakes over six furlongs for juvenile colts
October – Sun Chariot Stakes over a mile for fillies and mares
October – Champion Stakes over a mile and-a-quarter for three-year-olds and above
October – Dewhurst Stakes over seven furlongs for juveniles

What sets Newmarket apart from any of the other racecourses in Britain, though, is not only the mix of history that runs on the Heath, but also throughout the entire area, making it very much a racing community. Newmarket not only boasts the Tattersalls Bloodstock Sales, but some of the most famous studs – including both the Cheveley and National ones – as well as over fifty training stables. There is also the National Horseracing Museum located in the High Street, which contains memorabilia including the head of Persimmon, who won the Derby in 1899.

The Rowley Mile was closed toward the late 1990s, with racing switched across the Devil's Dyke – which separates the two courses – to the July Course, as Newmarket set about improving its facilities. The Queen opened the new Millennium Grandstand in 2000, and the impressive modern skyline advertises the racecourses continuing progress.

SANDOWN PARK – Surrey

FLAT

A right-handed, oval track, one mile five furlongs long and galloping, with an uphill finish. There is a separate five-furlong course in the centre of the track.

The first meeting was staged at Sandown Park in 1875, with its founders keen to start off with a mixed three-day fixture, focusing on a hunting and military theme. The mix of both Flat and Jumps racing on the same card is very rare throughout the world, and a tradition that has been kept to this day, with the end of Jumps meeting (formerly the Whitbread) at Sandown in April.

In 1886, Sandown hosted the first-ever race worth £10,000 in England, the Eclipse Stakes – named after one of the great thoroughbreds to win numerous King's Plates between 1769-70. The Group One Eclipse Stakes is still the biggest race run on the Flat at Sandown, but has been joined over the years by these Group races:

April – Classic Trial over a mile-and-a-quarter for three-year-olds
April – Mile Stakes over a mile for older horses
April – Gordon Richards Stakes over a mile-and-a-quarter for older horses

GREAT COURSES

CHAPTER 7

GREAT COURSES

Left
A Scenic view of The Curragh racecourse in County Kildare.

June – Henry II Stakes over two miles for older horses
June – Temple Stakes over five furlongs for three-year-olds and above
June – Brigadier Gerard Stakes over a mile-and-a-quarter for older horses
July – Champagne Sprint Stakes over five furlongs for three-year-olds and above
August – Solario Stakes over seven furlongs for juveniles

The National Hunt programme is also one of the best in the country, attracting quality jumpers whose skills are tested against the three Railway Fences in the back straight. The racecourse's stiff uphill finish contributes towards the tight finishes that are seen here, as some horses run out of steam as others begin to get going.

The Grade Three Gold Cup over three miles five furlongs – first run in 1957 – used to be the main race over the jumps, but has been passed in recent years by the Grade One Tingle Creek Trophy Chase.

This race always brings together the two-mile chasers around, acting as a stepping-stone towards the Queen Mother Champion Chase at the Cheltenham Festival. The other quality events that earn Grade status are:
December – Winter Novices' Hurdle over two and-a-half miles
December – Henry VIII Novice Stakes over two miles
January – Tolworth Hurdle over two miles
February – Scilly Isles Novices' Chase over two-and-a-half miles
April – Celebration Chase over two miles

The racecourse has always proved popular with the public, as its location offers different options of transport – Heathrow Airport and the M25 are close by – with regular trains from London. It also plays host to the ever-popular Variety Club Day, which raises money for children's charities, bringing together a host of celebrities as well as top-class racing. The Club had its 47th annual Race Day in 2005, and contributes towards Sandown Park being one of the most family-orientated racecourses in Britain.

IRELAND

THE CURRAGH – Co. Kildare

FLAT

A right-handed galloping, horseshoe shaped track – with three separate chutes – measuring two miles long. There is also an adjoining straight mile course, where the final three furlongs are uphill.

The origins of the Curragh – meaning 'place of the running horse' – stretch back as far as the third century, when it is reported to have played host to chariot racing. The racecourse itself, however, emerged in the early 1700s, when the lord lieutenant and his men used the area to race their horses in the King's Plates.

Right
The enclosure at the Kildare Hunt Steeplechases at Punchestown racecourse, 1913.

Right inset top
The Powers Gold Label Irish Grand National Steeple Chase run at Fairyhouse, 2003.

Right inset below
The Deloitte Novice Hurdle run at Leopardstown racecourse, 2004.

The Irish Turf Club – the governing body in Ireland – was formed around the 1760s in Kildare, south of Dublin, and it was from this point, that the Curragh became the headquarters for horse racing in Ireland.

The Curragh stages all five Irish Classics, with the first of those – the Irish Derby over a mile-and-a-half – founded in 1866. The Irish Oaks over the same distance followed in 1895, with the St. Leger, over a mile-and-a-three-quarters beginning in 1915. The final two Classics to be founded – now the first to be run – arrived soon after, with the Two Thousand Guineas in 1921, and the One Thousand Guineas in 1922.

There are several other significant races staged at the racecourse every year including the following Group One events:

May – Tattersalls Gold Cup over a mile-and-a-quarter for older horses
June – Pretty Polly Stakes over a mile-and-a-quarter for three-year-olds and above
August – Phoenix Stakes over six furlongs for juveniles
September – Moyglare Stud Stakes over seven furlongs for juvenile fillies
September – National Stakes over seven furlongs for juveniles

The Curragh plays a similar role to Newmarket in England, as it is also responsible for a huge part of the Irish Bloodstock industry, and has several stud farms, including the National Stud. There are also numerous training grounds, stables and gallops to be found within the vast area, which is located amongst superb scenery.

FAIRYHOUSE – near Dublin
FLAT AND NATIONAL HUNT

A right-handed, slightly undulating track, a mile-and-a-three quarters long.

Racing got underway at Fairyhouse in 1848, on an area of land opposite the current racecourse, where point-to-point racing between the flags was staged.

The race most associated with Fairyhouse is the Irish Grand National, which is run over three miles, five furlongs every spring as part of the Easter Festival, and was founded in 1870. Fairyhouse has grown in stature during recent times, bringing with it other races of significance to the Irish calendar, including these Grade One events:

April – Gold Cup over two-and-a-half miles
November – Royal Bond Novice Hurdle over two miles
November – Drinmore Novice Chase over two-and-a-half miles
November – Hatton's Grace Hurdle over two-and-a-half miles

The racecourse was predominately a National Hunt venue until the 1970s, when Flat racing was introduced. Fairyhouse has been modernised in the past thirty years, with the introduction of new facilities, the new grandstand in 1989, The Powers Gold Label Stand, with the Jameson Stand following ten years later. There is a nice balance of old and new at Fairyhouse, as the course is located a short drive away from Dublin, and sits in a wide area of open countryside, attracting numerous family spectators to create a warm atmosphere.

LEOPARDSTOWN – Foxrock, Dublin
FLAT AND NATIONAL HUNT

A left-handed, level track, a mile-and-three-quarters long, with an uphill finish.

The first meeting to take place at Leopardstown was in 1888, when 50,000 locals from Dublin got together. The actual racecourse was built by Captain George Quinn, who based it around Sandown Park in England.

Set in suburban Dublin, Leopardstown has thrived since 1967, when it was officially purchased from the Racing Board, and now features not only first-class facilities, but also the racing to match. In 2005, they staged no fewer than ten Grade One events under National Hunt Rules, as well as two Group One races on the Flat, as follows:

National Hunt
January – Arkle Challenge Cup Novice Chase over two miles one furlong
January – Champion Hurdle over two miles
February – Deloitte Novice Hurdle over two miles-and-a-quarter
February – Moriarty Novice Chase over two miles five furlongs
February – Hennessy Gold Cup over three miles
December – Durkan Novice Chase over two miles one furlong
December – Paddy Power Chase over two miles one furlong
December – Ascon/Rochon Novice Chase over three miles
December – Lexus Chase over three miles
December – Festival Hurdle over two miles

Flat
September – Matron Stakes over a mile for fillies and mares
September – Irish Champion Stakes over a-mile-and-a-quarter for three-year-olds and above

PUNCHESTOWN – Co. Kildare
NATIONAL HUNT

A right-handed, oval track, two miles long, with a run-in of three-and-half-furlongs.

There is also a bank course three miles long.

Racing got underway at Punchestown in 1824, over two days on open countryside, where the main obstacles for horses were stonewalls and bank sides. This is one of the features, which make this racecourse unique and one of the great tracks, as it has retained the bank course, used every April to run the Ladies Perpetual Cup and the La Touche Cup.

GREAT COURSES

CHAPTER 7

FIRST DERBY
1875
DERBY
2006

In 1850, the Kildare Hunt was held, and the popularity of this two-day fixture grew over the years to the point where the racecourse began constructing stands for spectators in 1960. It was also around this period that proper fences and hurdles were introduced, leading to a separate course being laid out.

Punchestown has maintained its old traditions, staging the Punchestown Gold Cup – originally the first steeplechase run there – as well as modernising its facilities, including the Panoramic Stand. The future looks very prosperous for Punchestown, with the Festival in April, growing enormously in recent times, becoming the 'Irish Cheltenham'. In 1988, only three Grade One races were run at the Festival, in comparison to the ten Grade One events run in 2005, consisting of the following:

April – Champion Novice Hurdle over two miles
April – Champion Chase over two miles
April – Punchestown Gold Cup over three miles one furlong
April – Champion Bumper over two miles
April – Champion Four-Year-Old Hurdle over two miles
April – Swordlestown Cup Novice Chase over two miles
April – Champion Stayers Hurdle over two miles
April – Champion Hurdle over two miles
April – Champion Novice Hurdle over two-and-a-half miles
April – John Durkan Punchestown Chase over two-and-a-half miles

FRANCE

LONGCHAMP – Paris

FLAT

A right-handed, oval track, with four separate courses, three of which sit in the middle of the large track.

In August 1854, the French governing body authorised a racetrack to be built in the Bois de Boulogne, a park to the west of Paris. Three years later, the first meeting took place amongst a huge audience, said to be near 100,000, including Napoleon III. Horse racing here became an instant success, with all walks of society making their way to the track down the River Seine.

In 1914, Longchamp staged the Grand Prix de Paris – originally run in 1862 – although racing was put on hold for the war, before getting underway again five years later. The following year saw the introduction of the Prix de l'Arc de Triomphe over a mile-and-a-half, which is currently the richest race in Europe. The popularity of 'The Arc' grew hugely, and the racecourse had to keep up with the increasing demand for seats, so in 1962, a new stand was built, before even more modern facilities were added. 'Arc' day in early October draws similarities to Ladies Day at Royal Ascot, where a sea of fashionable hats is guaranteed to be on parade.

Longchamp is awash with fantastic races every year, staging an incredible sixteen Group One events in 2005, including the following:

April – Prix Ganay over a mile-and-a-quarter for older horses
May – Poule d'Essai des Pouliches (One Thousand Guineas) over a mile for three-year-old fillies
May – Poule d'Essai des Poulains (Two Thousand Guineas) over a mile for three-year-old colts
May – Prix d'Ispahan over one mile one furlong for older horses
July – Grand Prix de Paris over one-and-a-half-miles for three-year-olds
September – Prix du Moulin over a mile for three-year-olds and above
October – Prix Marcel Boussac over a mile for juvenile fillies
October – Prix de L'Abbaye over five furlongs for juveniles and above
October – Grand Criterium over seven furlongs for juveniles

The racecourse is now compared to the best in America, with its immaculate appearance and surroundings, including fields for picnics, statues of great horses, beautifully cut hedges, souvenir stands, and the low trees that cover the paddock.

UNITED STATES OF AMERICA

CHURCHILL DOWNS – Kentucky

FLAT

A left-handed, oval level circuit, one-mile long, with tight turns. The turf course is positioned inside the dirt track.

After touring across Europe in 1872-73, Colonel M. Lewis Clark returned to Louisville, Kentucky with an idea to build a racetrack, and put his plans into motion during 1874. In order to raise the funds for the project, Clark sold membership subscriptions to the track, which raised over $30,000.

The first meeting took place in May 1875, and the first running of the Kentucky Derby – over a mile-and-a-half – was born, an idea Clark had taken from England on his visit. The Kentucky Oaks followed the Kentucky Derby along with the Clark Handicap – based on the English Oaks and St. Leger – and all three races are still held at the track.

During the years 1894-95, a new grandstand was built, which was easily identifiable because of the two twin spires erected at the top of the roof – a symbol that is associated with the Kentucky Derby to this day. Such was the popularity of the 'Derby', that the Kentucky Jockey Club was formed in 1919, leading to three more racecourses being opened within the state.

In 1950, Churchill Downs became modernised, with more seats and boxes added to the stands and clubhouses. The 1950s also saw the first television broadcast of the 'Derby', as well as the first replays available to officials, while the racecourse itself benefited from its first sprinkler system.

Left top
Horses round the bend during the Arc De Triomphe at Longchamp racecourse, 1996.

Left bottom
Kentucky Oaks day at Churchill in 2006.

Right
Horses come out of the gate to start the 138th running of the Belmont Stakes at Belmont Park, 2006.

The Kentucky Derby – now run over a mile-and-a-quarter – is the first-leg of the American Triple Crown, and is accompanied at the track throughout the year by the following Grade 1 events:

May – Kentucky Oaks over one mile one furlong for three-year-old fillies
May – Humana Distaff Handicap over seven furlongs for older horses
May – Woodford Reserve Turf Classic over one mile one furlong (Turf)
June – Stephen Foster Handicap over one mile one furlong for three-year-olds and above

New management in the 1980s brought about further redevelopment, bringing the place up to scratch with fellow racetracks throughout the world. This helped to secure the Breeders' Cup, which has now been staged here five times.

The future of Churchill Downs looks healthy, as it is now part of the Churchill Downs Incorporated network of racetracks, which benefits from a wealth of investment.

BELMONT PARK – Elmont, New York

FLAT

A left-handed circuit, one-and-a-half miles long. The two turf tracks are positioned inside the dirt course.

Belmont Park first staged racing in 1905, and was named after the founder, August Belmont II. The race most associated with the course is the famous Belmont Stakes run over a mile-and-a-half, and first run in 1867 at Jerome Park, before moving to this venue after its first year.

The first fifteen years at Belmont Park included racing right-handed, or 'clockwise', which was done for the purposes of the upper class, viewing from the clubhouse. The racecourse saw numerous changes during the 1950s, including the seven-furlong straight which was introduced, and ran diagonally through the tracks. However, the entire track was deemed to be unsafe at the turn of the 1960s, and staged its last meeting there in October 1962 until the re-opening in may 1968.

During the redevelopment, a new turf course had been added to the inside circuit, along with the new Belmont Park grandstand which replaced the old, unsafe one, to the cost of over $30 million.

This made Belmont the largest racetrack in America, with a total capacity of 100,000. There are many attractions to the venue, including the picturesque paddock, equipped with a picnic area for race goers.

The race fixtures at Belmont Park are split into two segments, with the 'spring-summer meeting', lasting from May to July, and then the 'fall meeting' from September until October. Racing between this period is held at Saratoga from early July to early September. There are over twenty other major Grade One events to take place at Belmont Park during these meetings, which include the following races, all of which have in excess of $100,000 as first prize:

BELMONT PARK
12
11
10
9
8
7
6
5
4
3
2
UNITED PUETT

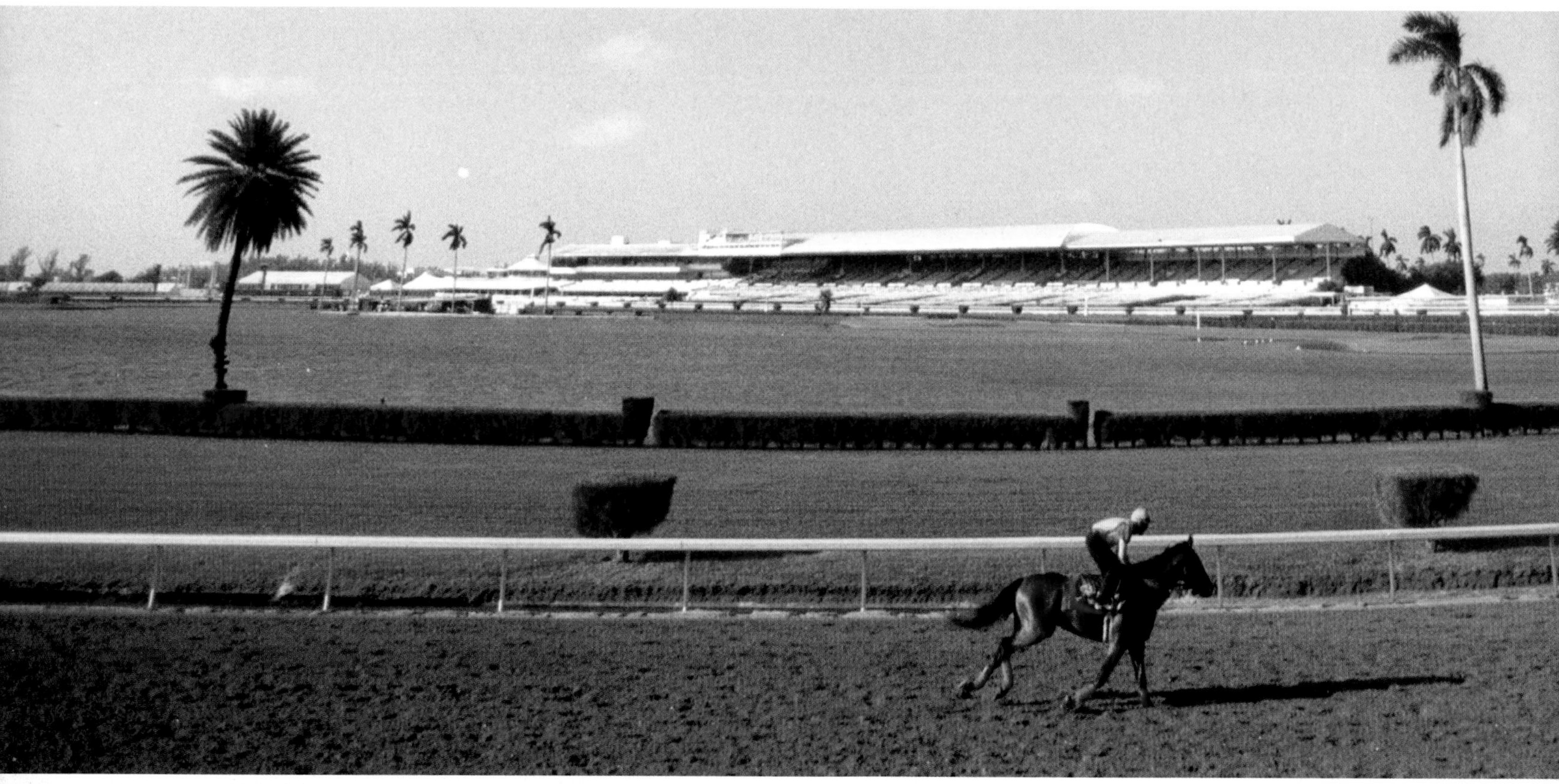

May – Metropolitan Handicap over a mile for three-year-olds and above (Dirt)
July – Suburban Handicap over a mile-and-a-quarter for three-year-olds and above (Dirt)
July – American Oaks over a mile-and-a-quarter for three-year-old fillies (Dirt)
September – Man O'War Stakes over one mile three furlongs for three-year-olds and above (Turf)
October – Flower Bowl Invitational over a mile-and-a-quarter for fillies and mares (Turf)
October – Joe Hirsch Turf Classic Invitational over a mile-and-a-half for three-year-olds and above (Turf)
October – Jockey Club Gold Cup over a mile-and-a-quarter for three-year-olds and above (Dirt)
October – Beldame Stakes over one mile one furlong for fillies and mares (Dirt)

Belmont Park has also staged the Breeders' Cup four times since 1990, and continues to attract the very best thoroughbreds from all over the world.

GULFSTREAM PARK – Florida

FLAT

A left-handed, level circuit, one mile one furlong long around the outside dirt track, and a turf course on the inside.

Gulfstream Park is a relatively new racecourse, opening its gates for the first meeting in February 1939 for a four-day fixture that attracted 18,000 on the opening day.

Seven years later, the racecourse introduced one if its first major races in the shape of the Gulfstream Park Handicap over a mile-and-a-quarter, before adding the Florida Derby over one mile, one furlong six years later – both on dirt. Both races are still currently staged, as is the Donn Handicap (Dirt) over one mile, one furlong introduced a few years later.

1952 was also the same year the clubhouse was added to the old grandstand before being enlarged in 1961. This period also welcomed changes to the centre of the track, with the turf course being installed inside the dirt track in 1959, before the world's biggest totaliser board was planted in the middle a few years later.

The racecourse continued to update its facilities over the next 30 years, during which time, it attracted the Breeders' Cup Meeting, staging it three times since 1989. Three years later, the turf course was extended from a mile to a furlong further, with the introduction a new chute at the north end of the track.

The popularity of horse racing at Gulfstream Park hit new heights during the 1990s, as the racecourse consistently broke on-course wagering records, as well as setting its own benchmarks with attendance figures. Due to the ever-growing figures, a decision was made to upgrade the racecourse in an attempt to move forwards, and the track was closed for renovation in 2004.

This was to be the biggest project to take place in the history of Gulfstream Park. The new features included the lengthening and widening of the actual racetrack along with

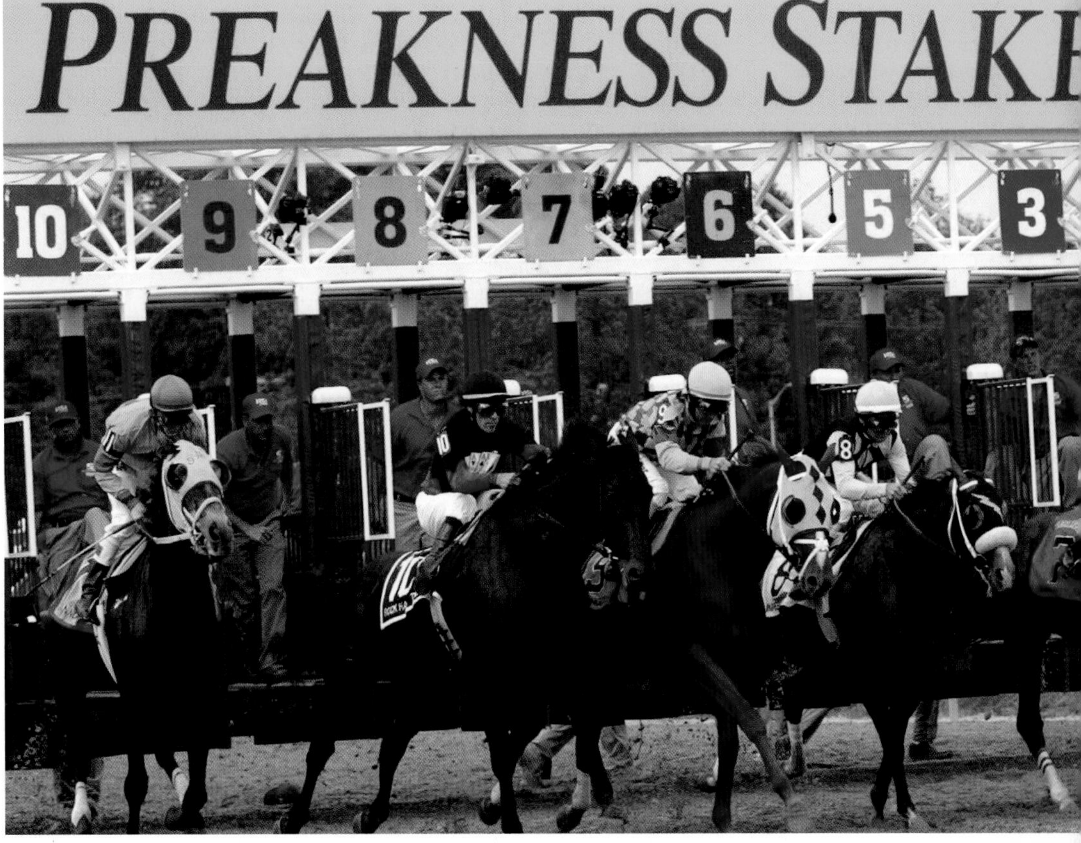

freshly laid surfaces, and a 300,000 square-foot four-story grandstand, along with retail and entertainment areas. The racecourse has also added plenty of trimmings such as new clubhouses, a fountain terrace, and arches to give it a Las Vegas appeal, which will attract an even bigger audience.

PIMLICO – Maryland

FLAT

A left-handed, level oval circuit, one mile long around the outside dirt track, with separate mile-and-a-quarter and six furlong chutes. There is an inner turf course seven furlongs in circumference.

Pimlico is the second oldest racecourse in the United States after Saratoga, founded in 1864, and engineered by General John Ellicott in1870. The idea for building the track came about during a dinner in Saratoga 1868, when the Maryland Governor, Oden Bowie, suggested a race to be run in two years' time to commemorate the evening. He kept his word, building the racecourse on seventy acres of land, which had been occupied by English settlers in 1669 – known then as 'Pemblicoe' – and the Dinner Party Stakes got underway on 25th October 1870.

There was a piece of uphill land located in the centre of the track, which was used by trainers to gain a advantageous viewpoint, and led to the racetrack being later referred to as 'Old Hilltop'. However, the hill was removed in 1938, as it presented a hazard to the new television cameras. The centre of the course continued to be popular with the fashion-conscious, a theme that has continued to this day.

In 1873, the first running of the famous Preakness Stakes took place, which now forms the second-leg of the American Triple-Crown. The race was to change in distance over the years before settling at just short of a mile-and-a-quarter. One of the unique features about Pimlico takes place every year after the Preakness, when the winning colours are painted onto a horse-figures weather vane, standing at the winner's enclosure, inside the track.

The Preakness was also run at different venues from 1889 before returning to Pimlico in 1909, where it has been staged ever since. During the period of absence from Pimlico, Flat racing was put on hold. The introduction of steeplechase racing temporarily emerged, before Flat racing returned and a new era was born.

Pimlico later became the first racecourse to use electric starting stalls, and has prospered despite experiencing storms, a fire, an anti-gambling motion which saw horse racing banned in other states, and the Great Depression of the 1930s.

Pimlico now stages two other Grade One events to accompany the Preakness Stakes, both of which are also run on dirt: Pimlico Special over just short of a mile-and-a-quarter for older horses, and the Frank J de Francis Memorial Dash over six furlongs for three-year-olds and above.

Above left
Lemon Drop Kidd runs on the track in an early morning workout before the Breeders Cup at the Gulfstream Park racecourse.

Above right
Horses break the starting gate at the 129th Preakness Stakes at the Pimlico racecourse, 2004.

Right
Glen Boss on Makybe Diva wins the Melbourne Cup for the third year in a row during The Melbourne Cup Carnival at Flemington, 2005.

Far right
Horses taking the final turn of the Providencia Stakes Turf race with San Gabriel Mountains in the background at Santa Anita Park, 2005.

SANTA ANITA – California

FLAT

A left-handed, level circuit, one mile long around the outside dirt track, with an inside turf course seven furlongs long. The uphill turf course crosses part of the dirt course in six-and-a-half furlong races.

Like Gulfstream Park, this Californian racecourse is relatively new – despite being one of the oldest in the state – founded in 1934 by Elias Jackson Baldwin, who named it after his daughter Anita. The first meeting took place on Christmas Day of that year, and two months later came the introduction of the famous Santa Anita Handicap over a mile-and-a-quarter on dirt – later to be won by Seabiscuit.

Santa Anita instantly became a major hit not only with race goers but also celebrities, attracting the likes of Charlie Chaplin, Bing Crosby and Fred Astaire.

The course was closed to race goers between 1942 and 1945, although, it kept its doors open to house 20,000 Japanese Americans who were awaiting relocation. The turf course was added in 1953, before major redevelopments took place in the 1960s, including the grandstand being updated, as racing continued on the up throughout the 1970s and 80s. In 1984, it played host to the equestrian games during the Olympics, and two years later staged the first of its three Breeders' Cups – with the others taking place in 1993 and 2003.

Santa Anita continues to thrive, staging some of the richest races in the United States, including the Grade One Yellow Ribbon Stakes over a mile-and-a-quarter for three-year-olds and above in October.

AUSTRALIA

FLEMINGTON – Melbourne

FLAT

A left-handed, pear-shaped level turf track, with a circumference of 2,312 metres, and an adjoining six furlongs – known as the 'Straight Six'.

Horse racing has taken place in Melbourne, besides the Maribyrnong River, since 1840, when it was known as the Melbourne Racecourse. 20 years later, the racecourse was handed the new title 'Flemington' – originating from a local town and hotel, which may have derived from an early settler, Robert Fleming.

In 1854, the Victoria Turf Club decided to start staging an autumn and spring meeting, before introducing the famous Melbourne Cup – a two mile handicap – seven year later, in 1861. The race gathered momentum during the period from the gold rush era, through to the 1880s, as Melbourne attracted more people, and the event became a fashionable social gathering, with crowds of 100,000 assembling.

The racecourse developed hugely in the 20th century, with training facilities improving, and the introduction of the

the hill stand
the lawn stand
13

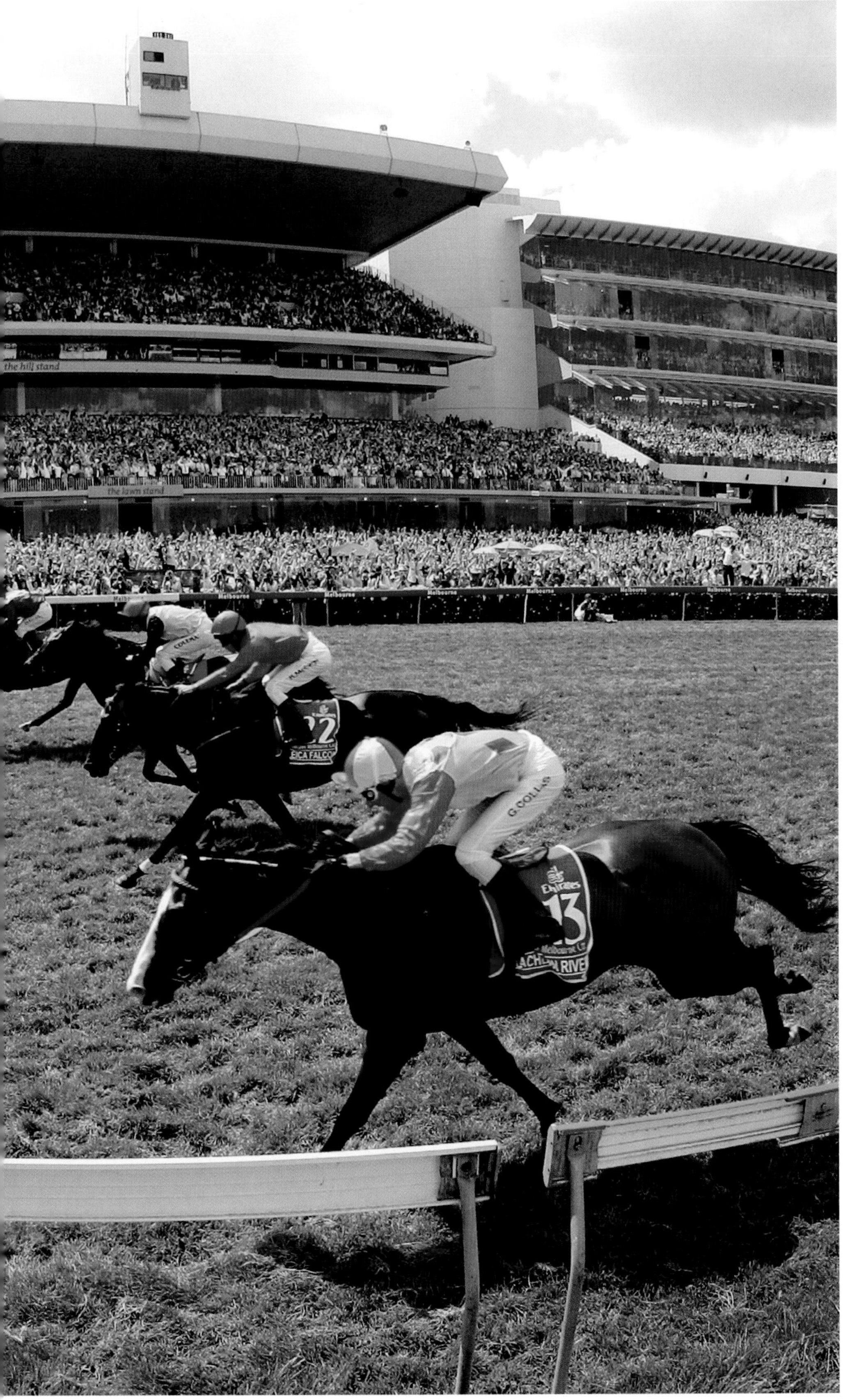

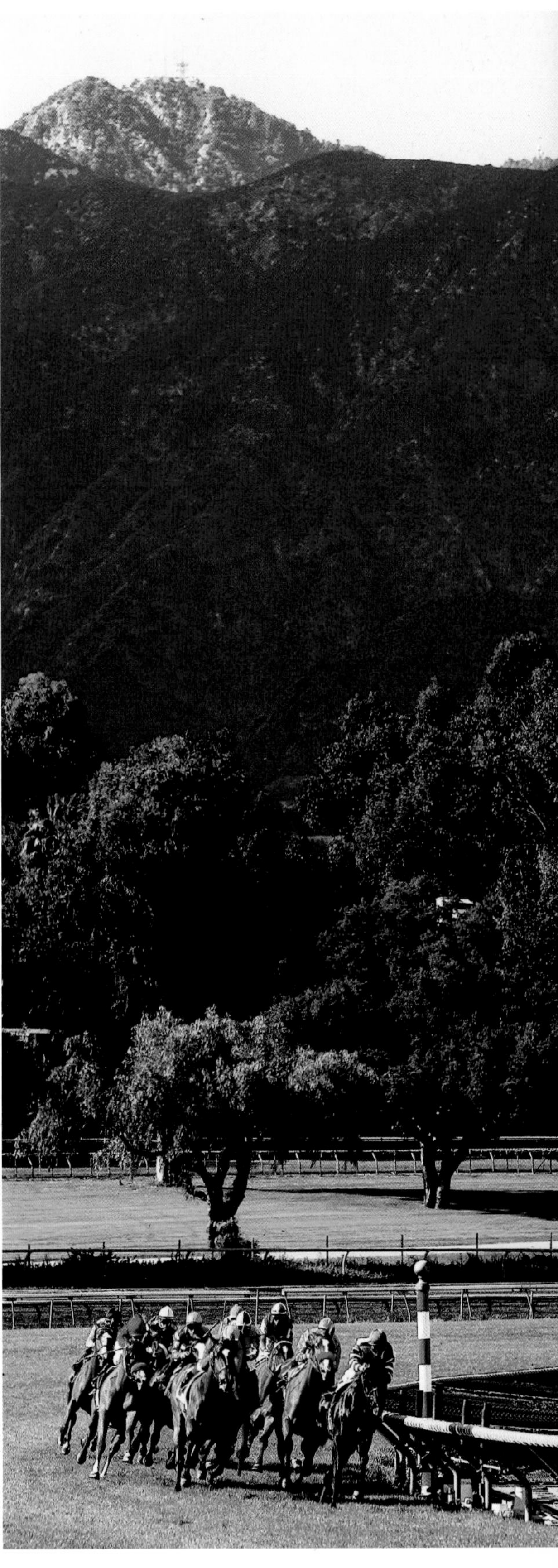

タイム2.08.7
4F 50.4
3F 37.6

Left
The Japan Cup Dirt at Fuchu, 2004.

'Birdcage', which allows the public to get close up to the horses, in an area full of attractive lawns and hedges.

A batch of additional Group One events has also emerged to attract the best horses, alongside the Melbourne Cup, including:

February – Lightning Stakes over five furlongs for three-year-olds and above
February – Guineas over a mile for three-year-olds
March – Newmarket Handicap over six furlongs for three-year-olds and above
March – Produce Stakes over seven furlongs for juveniles
March – Australian Cup over a mile-and-a-quarter for three-year-olds and above
October – Victoria Derby over a mile-and-a-half for two and three-year-olds
October – Mackinnon Stakes over a mile-and-a-quarter for three-year-olds and above
October – Salinger Stakes over six furlongs for three-year-olds and above
November – Crown Oaks over a mile-and-a-half for three-year-old fillies

Flemington has seen the facilities change over the years, and one of the most significant came in the year 2000, when a spanking new $45 million grandstand was opened to cope with the growing attendances – approaching 125,000. The racecourse has moved forwards quickly in a short time, but hasn't forgotten its past, as a bronze statue of the great Phar Lap, reminds modern day race goers of the 1930 Melbourne Cup winner.

JAPAN

TOKYO – Fuchu, Tokyo

FLAT

A left-handed, level oval circuit, with the outside turf track measuring 2,083 metres long, and the inside dirt course 1,899 metres in circumference. There is also a steeplechase track inside the dirt circuit.

Not many racecourses can offer their country's biggest mountain as part of the scenery – Mount Fuji – making Tokyo not only the biggest track in Japan, but also one of the greatest in the world.

Situated 25 kilometres west of Tokyo, this premier racecourse was not founded until 1933, but soon made an instant splash by hosting the Japan Derby (Tokyo Yushun). This race was based upon the English version, also run over a mile-and-a-half for three-year-olds, and was originally run at Meguro Racecourse in Tokyo, before moving across the city.

Tokyo racecourse built on the acquirement of that race to firmly establish itself in a short period of time, and there has been redevelopment work since the Millennium to update their facilities. These include significant extensions to the grandstand, as well as altering the racetrack itself, with the

Right
Runners make their round the Happy Valley Racecourse, 2005.

Right inset top
The world's richest race the Dubai World Cup held at Nad Al Sheba in the United Arab Emirates, 2006.

Right inset below
Shane Dye of New Zealand enters the track from the tunnel during trackwork for the Cathay Pacific International Races at Sha Tin, 2005.

home stretch lengthened by 25 metres and an upgraded large screen (11m x 60m) to be installed.

The growth of Tokyo racecourse has led to five hundred races being run over 48 weekends every year, including the famous Grade One Japan Cup over a mile-and-a-half on turf, which was introduced in 1981. There are also another six Grade One races that take place at the racecourse including:

February – February Stakes over a mile for older horses (dirt)
May – NHK Mile Cup over a mile for three-year-olds (turf)
May – Yushun Himba (Oaks) over a mile-and-a-half for three-year-olds (turf)
June – Yasuda Kinen over a mile for three-year-olds and above (turf)
October – Tenno Sho over a mile-and-a-quarter for three-year-olds and above (turf)
November – Japan Cup over a mile-and-a-quarter for three-year-olds and above (dirt)

UNITED ARAB EMIRATES

NAD AL SHEBA - Dubai

FLAT

A left-handed level track, with the outside dirt track measuring 2,254 metres long, and the inner turf track 2,121 metres in circumference. There are three separate chutes at the 2,000, 1,600 and 1,200 metre starting points.

Nad Al Sheba is one of the newest racecourses in the world, but has rapidly become one of the greatest, featuring all the modern facilities seen elsewhere around the globe. Not only does it house some of the finest training resources, but also a spectacular floodlit eighteen-hole golf course, located in the centre of the track.

The racecourse was founded by His Highness Sheikh Maktoum bin Rashid Al Maktoum and built on an area bordering the desert, with the first meeting taking place in 1992. The venue staged the world-class race it fully deserved in 1996, when the inaugural running the Grade One Dubai World Cup took place, now the richest race on the planet. The race itself, over a mile-and-a-quarter for older horses on dirt, is part of a fantastic card staged as a climax to the Dubai Carnival, which runs throughout the winter.

The other Group One races, which support this World Cup card, are:

Dubai Golden Shaheen over six furlongs for three-year-olds and above (Dirt)
Dubai Sheema Classic over a mile-and-a-half for older horses (Turf)
Dubai Duty Free over one mile one furlong for older horses (Turf)

Nad Al Sheba has continued to progress in recent years, with the Maktoum Grandstand being updated in 1993, 1999 and 2000, along with the opening of the Millennium Grandstand in 2001, which is one of the finest anywhere, offering some breathtaking views.

OTHER MAJOR RACECOURSES OF THE WORLD

HONG KONG

HAPPY VALLEY - Right-handed

Built in 1845 due to the demand from British-based citizens in Hong Kong with an appetite for watching horse racing, Happy Valley held its first meeting a year later in 1846. The area chosen to build the course on Hong Kong Island was a reclaimed marshland, but it was the only piece of flat land available, forcing rice growing to be forbidden in nearby areas.

The racecourse suffered a tragedy in 1918, when a fire killed just fewer than six hundred people – the highest number associated with such tragedy in the country's history.

The Hong Kong Jockey Club, which was founded in 1884 before becoming a professional body in 1971, and whose premises are on the course itself, controls Happy Valley. In 1973, the introduction of night racing at Happy Valley came about, proving enormously popular with the locals, creating an electric atmosphere amongst the bright lights.

The horseracing season at Happy Valley runs from September through to June, with most meetings taking place on Wednesday evenings and the occasional weekends.

SHA-TIN - Right-handed

The largest of Hong Kong's two racecourses – consisting of the Penfold Park Complex – which has grown to a capacity of 85,000. Built in 1978, and equipped with modern facilities, such as an equine hospital and gallops, it usually stages meetings at the weekends on both turf and dirt. There are several major Group One events, which take place here, including the Hong Kong Cup over

Far left
The Breeders' Cup held at Woodbine racetrack, 1996.

Left
Spectators dine in the open air as the horses go by at Baden Baden racecourse, Germany, 1978.

a mile-and-a-quarter, Hong Kong Mile, Hong Kong Vase over a mile-and-a-half, and the Hong Kong Sprint over five furlongs – all taking place on turf during December.

CANADA

WOODBINE – Left-handed

Canada's premier racecourse, located on the north-western outskirts of Toronto, Ontario, staged its first meeting in June 1956. It is a unique venue, in that it is the only North American racetrack to offer both thoroughbred and standard bred racing on the same day – held the first harness fixture on New Year's Day 1994. The track inherited its name from the Old Woodbine racecourse on the east side of Toronto, which held race meetings until 1993.

Woodbine became the first racetrack to stage the Breeders' Cup outside of the United States, playing host to the event in 1996. The most popular race associated with the racecourse is the Grade One Canadian International over a mile-and-a-half on turf. It also stages the Atto Mile and the E P Taylor Stakes over a mile-and-a-quarter, both Grade One races on turf.

GERMANY

BADEN-BADEN (IFFEZHEIM) – Left-handed

Horse racing at Iffezheim racecourse in Baden Baden dates back to 1858, and was built to accompany the town's casino, as a form of entertainment during the daytime. The track is located towards the southwest of Germany, situated between the Rhine and the Black Forest, and is the most popular horseracing venue in the country, as it also stages steeplechase races.

It was not until 1905 that horse racing started to become popular here, as a result of His Royal Highness Friedrich I visiting the track, along with guests who helped inject more finance. This led to a new influx of race goers, and betting taxes were reduced, increasing turnover enormously. This new injection of capital helped fund the main stands and other facilities including the weighing room in 1912.

The racetrack was closed for periods during both wars, before staging racing again in 1950, but it was not for another 27 years until the track received another makeover, when the club stands, gardens and entrance were developed.

The racing calendar here has been adjusted over the years, and now starts with the Spring Meeting (end of May/start of June), followed by the Grand Festival Week (end of August/start of September), before finishing with the Sales & Racing Festival (end of October).

The main race to be staged at Baden-Baden is the Group One Grosser Preis von Baden over a mile-and-a-half for three-year-olds and above, and has become one of the most prestigious races in Europe for middle-distance horses.

Right
Willie Carson (second right) on Nashwan, races towards the finishing post during the 2000 Guineas at Newmarket, 1989.

The term "a great race" can be defined in two ways. There is the title itself, such as the Derby, Grand National or Cheltenham Gold Cup. These races are recognised throughout the world and are steeped in history. The second revolves around the actual running of the race itself, where the best thoroughbreds go stride for stride in a battle to the winning post.

Perhaps the two elements need to be combined so that a great race requires two great horses fighting it out in a famous race; nobody remembers a thrilling, four-horse photo finish in the last race on a Monday at a minor track!

Then the occasion itself must be considered, so the moment leaves its mark in racing history. A great race will instantly remind the enthusiast of their whereabouts upon witnessing such an outstanding contest, and the following are amongst the most memorable within the sport's long history.

CHAPTER 8 GREAT RACES

ENGLAND

FLAT

THE TWO THOUSAND GUINEAS

Group One, three-year-old colts and fillies only, one mile
NEWMARKET

The Two Thousand Guineas is the first of the Five English Classics to be run every season, taking place on the first day of the two-day Guineas meeting in early-May. It was founded in 1809, when it was won by Wizard, and is run over the same course and distance as the One Thousand Guineas. As with the female version of the event, there is usually little form on show for students to work with, being an early season race, and the previous year's juvenile runs are the best guides.

The longest priced winner of this prestige race came in 1961, when Rockavon won at 50-1, with the last odds-on winner being Zafonic in 1993.

Some memorable Two Thousand Guineas have taken place, with perhaps the 1971 race amongst the best. It brought together three special colts in Brigadier Gerard, Mill Reef and My Swallow, in which the former – trained by Major Dick Hern – came out on top. The Major also trained the last winner of this race to go on and win the Derby, Nashwan in 1989.

The following colts all managed to go one better, however, in recording the Triple Crown – adding the Derby and St. Leger – a feat which has become even more scarce in recent years:

Left
The racehorse Pretty Polly, who won the One Thousand Guineas, the Oaks and the St. Leger.

Right
Willie Carson (left), riding the Queen's horse Dunfermline to victory in the Oaks at Epsom in 1977.

Far right
Edward Smith Stanley, the Twelfth Earl of Derby, a patron of horse racing who instituted both the Oaks in 1779 and the Derby in 1780.

1853 West Australian, **1865** Gladiateur, **1866** Lord Lyon, **1886** Ormonde, **1891** Common, **1893** Isinglass, **1897** Galtee More, **1899** Flying Fox, **1900** Diamond Jubilee, **1903** Rock Sand, **1915** Pommern, **1917** Gay Crusader, **1918** Gainsborough, **1935** Bahram, **1970** Nijinsky

THE ONE THOUSAND GUINEAS

Group One, Three-year-old fillies, one mile,
NEWMARKET

The One Thousand Guineas is the youngest of the five English Classics to be run during the Flat season, being founded in 1814 and won by Charlotte.

Run over a straight mile at the Rowley Course, Newmarket, on the second day of the two-day Guineas Meeting in early-May, it is always a competitive affair, regularly attracting a big field of runners.

The race has seen its fair share of fancied winners, with numerous odds-on shots winning. Bosra Sham was the last such winner in 1996, whereas the longest-priced came in 1918, when Ferry won at 50-1.

Some of the best fillies to have won this event include the following, all of whom managed to secure the Triple Crown (with the Oaks and St. Leger) during the same season:

1868 Formosa, **1871** Hannah, **1874** Apology, **1892** La Fleche, **1902** Sceptre, **1904** Pretty Polly, **1942** Sun Chariot, **1955** Meld, **1985** Oh So Sharp.

THE OAKS

Group One, three-year-old fillies, one mile four furlongs,
EPSOM

Founded in 1779 by Lord Derby, who named it after his house, the first running of the event was won by a filly named Bridget. It is the third of the English Classics, and is run over a mile-and-a-half around Epsom Downs, on the first day of the two-day meeting at Epsom in early June.

There have not been many shocks in this historic event, with the longest priced winners coming in 1833 and 1991, with Vespa and Jet Ski Lady respectively, both

priced at 50-1. The last odds-on winner was Reams Of Verse in 1997, trained by Henry Cecil, who also won the race seven times between 1985 and 2000.

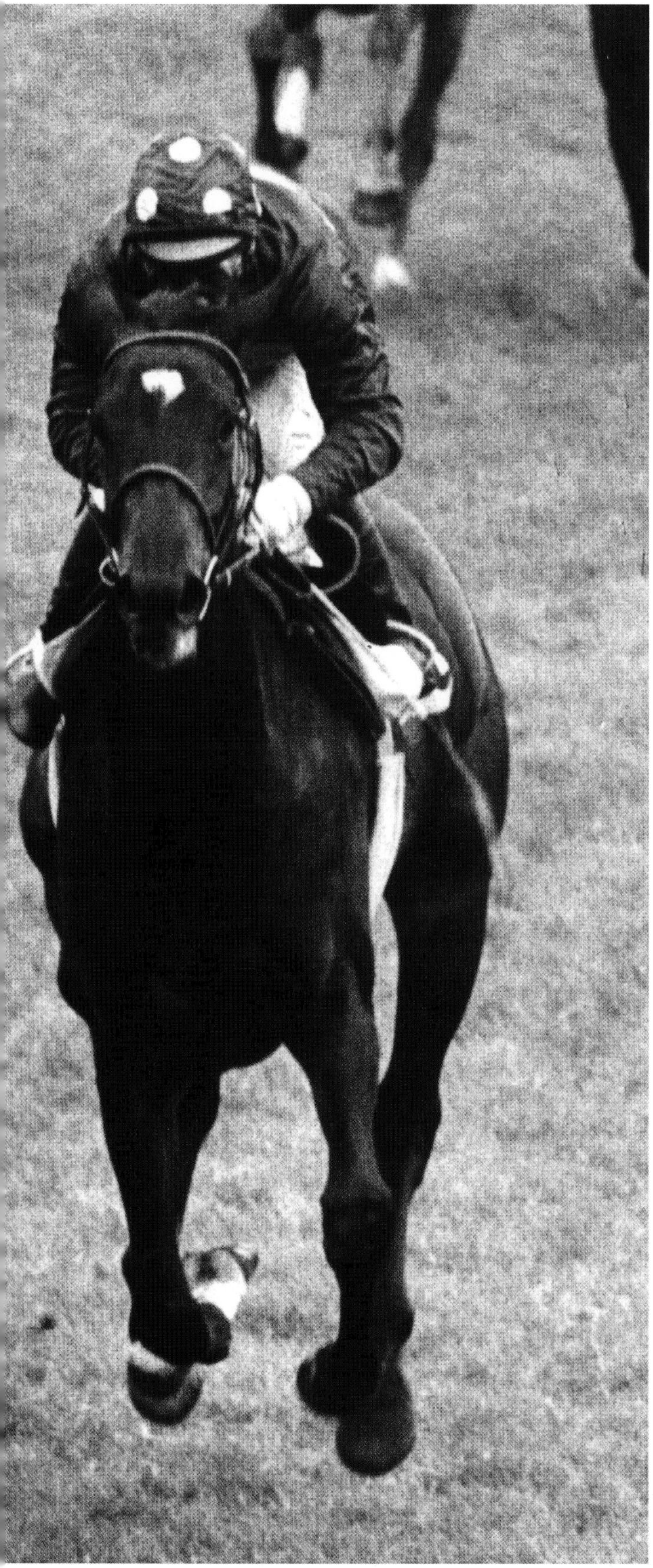

One of the most popular winners of The Oaks was in 1977, when Dunfermline won for her owner, Her Majesty The Queen, during her Silver Jubilee year. One of the best recent winners was Ouija Board, who won at Epsom in 2004 before landing the Irish Oaks, Breeders' Cup, and then the Hong Kong Vase a year later.

Left
Shergar 10 lengths clear beats the rest of the field to win the Derby at Epsom in 1981.

THE DERBY

Group One, three-year-old colts and fillies, one mile four furlongs,

EPSOM

A year after The Oaks was first run for fillies in 1780, Lord Derby introduced another race open to both fillies and colts, a race which was to become one of the leading events for thoroughbreds in the history of horse racing.

The title of The Derby has been replicated in many countries, such as the Kentucky Derby in the United States, with almost every major horseracing nation now staging its own version.

The first Derby was run over a mile for the first prize of 1,075 guineas – won by Diomed – and was raced over that distance until 1784 before being altered to that of The Oaks – a mile-and-a-half – at which it remains today.

The great race has witnessed many memorable moments since the inaugural running, including in 1801 when Eleanor became the first filly to win. Then in 1884, there was the first dead heat in the event between Harvester and St Gatien, before the race itself was moved to Newmarket between 1915-18. Nine years after the end of the Great War, the BBC televised The Derby for the first time.

One of the greatest performances ever seen in this historic event came in 1981, when Shergar destroyed his rivals to win by a record-breaking ten lengths, as well as being the last odds-on winner. The race has also had its share of surprises, with the 1898 and 1913 races falling to 100-1 shots, Jeddah and Aboyeur, respectively.

THE ST. LEGER

Group One, three-year-olds, one mile six furlongs,

DONCASTER

The St. Leger is the last of the five English Classics to be run during the Flat season, as well as being of the English Triple Crown, along with the Two Thousand Guineas and The Derby. It is also the oldest of the Classics, having been staged for the first time in 1776, founded by Colonel Anthony St. Leger, an Irish soldier who later became Governor of St Lucia, and is held on the final day of the four-day St. Leger meeting at Doncaster in early September. The first winner was a horse called Allabaculia.

It was first run over two-miles on Cantley Common, a few miles from the current location of Town Moor, before being changed to its current format of a mile-and-three-quarters in 1813.

One of the races always referred to when the St. Leger is being discussed took place in 1850 – the race of the century – where Voltigeur originally dead-heated with an Irish colt, Russborough, before winning a run-off to decide matters a few hours later. Two days after that success, Voltigeur appeared in the Doncaster Cup and won again by beating a horse called The Flying Dutchman. To commemorate the St. Leger's 200th running in 1976, a larger-than-normal embroidered cap was

Right
Voltigeur, winner of the 1850 Derby.

Far right
Michael Roberts stands next to Mtoto after winning the King George VI and Queen Elizabeth Diamond Stakes at Ascot racecourse, 1987.

introduced and presented to the winning jockey. This presentation has become a unique tradition associated with the race.

The longest priced winner of the event was way back in 1822, when Theodore scored at 200-1, despite being lame before the race. In fact, it was said that there was more chance of the animal being put down before the off than going on to win it. There is a rich history of favourites landing the St. Leger, and Scorpion was the latest odds-on winner in 2005, becoming the 16th winning favourite since 1983. However, despite the race being popular with punters, its overall image has declined in recent years due to the current trend for breeding speedier horses, resulting in better quality middle-distance runners being entered elsewhere.

THE ECLIPSE

Group One, three-year-olds and above, one mile two furlongs,
SANDOWN PARK

This race is renowned for being the first Group One event in the calendar to bring together the mixed generations over middle distances, and has been run since 1886. It is run on the second day of the two-day Eclipse meeting at Sandown Park in early-July, and has become one of the longest-standing sponsored races in Britain.

Founded by Leopold de Rothschild, and named after the legendary 18th century racehorse Eclipse, during the same year as an astronomical eclipse, it was won for the first time by Bendigo. A record 30,000 people witnessed that inaugural running, and the £10,000 first prize was also the first five-figure sum to be offered.

There have been some thrilling finishes during the race's long history, including the dead-heat between Neil Gow and Lemberg in 1910, as well as the superb victories by Sadler's Wells and Pebbles in the mid-eighties. But the 1987 renewal was arguably one of the best, as it brought together the Derby winner, Reference Point, the Group One French winner Triptych, and the late-maturing Mtoto. During the climax of the race, Reference Point and Mtoto were going stride-for-stride and neither gave way until the latter just got in front to land the race.

13 years later, two Royal Ascot winners came together to battle it out up the hill. On that day in 2000, the 'Iron Horse', Giant's Causeway, fought back courageously to get the better of Kalanisi, demonstrating that this ten-furlong event can still draw the best horses to provide exciting clashes.

GREAT RACES

CHAPTER 8

Right
Pat Eddery gives his mount Grundy a pat as he is led in after winning the King George VI and Queen Elizabeth Diamond Stakes at Ascot in 1975

THE KING GEORGE VI AND QUEEN ELIZABETH DIAMOND STAKES

Group One, three-year-olds and above, one mile four furlongs.

ASCOT

One of the youngest Group One races to feature on the Flat racing calendar, this event was first run in 1951, when it was won by Supreme Court, and was then referred to as the Festival of Britain King George VI & Queen Elizabeth Stakes. The title of the race changed to its current name in 1975, when the word Diamond was allowed following the sponsorship of De Beers.

The race itself brings together mixed generations over a mile-and-a-half, and takes place on the second day of the three-day King George Meeting at the end of July.

The cream usually comes to the top in this event, and shocks are rare, with the biggest priced winner, Montaval, coming back in 1957. The last odds-on winner came in 2001, when Galileo won at 1-2, a year after Montjeu scored at odds of 1-3.

In the world of horse racing, one race pops up time and time again, especially when the King George VI is mentioned, and that is the race of the twentieth century, which took place at Ascot in 1975. The horses in question were the 1975 Derby and Irish Derby winner, Grundy, and the 1974 St. Leger winner, Bustino. As the pair entered the Ascot straight that day, battle took place, with neither horse giving an inch until Grundy showed special reserves to grind out the victory.

There have also been some popular winners of this race, including the likes of Nijinsky in 1970, Mill Reef in 1971, Brigadier Gerard in 1972, Dancing Brave in 1986, Lammtarra in 1995 and the dual-winner Swain in 1997 & 1998.

The race always appeals to the top owners, and Sheikh Mohammed has won it no fewer than seven times since 1990, while HH The Aga Khan IV has taken it three times, including with Shergar in 1981. He also won the event in 2005 with Azamour, when the race was run at Newbury, away from Ascot for the first time.

THE ASCOT GOLD CUP

Group One, four-year-olds and above, two miles four furlongs

ASCOT

Founded in 1807, the Gold Cup is Royal Ascot's most prestigous race and takes place on the third day of the five-day meeting – traditionally known as Ladies' Day. The race was first run over two miles – before being altered to its current distance of two-and-a-half miles – and was won by Master Jackey for a first prize of one hundred guineas. Due to the extreme distance over which it is now run, it is one of the most important races staged in Europe, a test of a thoroughbred's stamina, and regularly brings together a strong line-up of stayers.

The Gold Cup has witnessed some shocks in the past with two 20-1 winners in 1994 & 1999, while the last odds-on came in 1989, when Sadeem won at 8-11.

The Gold Cup was switched to Newmarket during both World Wars, when legendary jockey Gordon Richards notched a hat-trick of winners from 1942-44, although Lester Piggott was able to boast a total of 11 victories in the event.

The first horse to lift the Gold Cup twice was Anticipation in 1819, and the first to defend the title was Bizarre in 1825. There have been plenty of horses to have won the event more than once, including the likes of Sagaro three times from 1975-77, Le Moss in 1979-80, Ardross in 1981-82, Drum Taps 1992-93, and Kayf Tara in 1998 and 2000 for Godolphin, who have now taken the race four times.

THE JULY CUP

Group One, three-year-olds and above, six furlongs

NEWMARKET JULY COURSE

Along with the Golden Jubilee Stakes at Royal Ascot, the Nunthorpe Stakes at York, and the Sprint Cup at Haydock, the July Cup is one of the biggest sprints in Britain. The July Cup stands above the others, however, as it is viewed as the six-furlong Championship of Europe, with the winner becoming the Best European Sprinter in the International Classifications.

It is run on the final day of the three-day July Meeting at Newmarket, and was first run in 1876, won by Springfield who came back to double up the following year.

The only triple-winner of the event was Sundridge in 1902-04, although there have been several dual winners, including Abernant in 1949-50. Other popular winners of

10

5

the contest include, Diadem in 1919-20, Right Boy in 1958-59, Thatching in 1979, Ajdal in 1987, and Cadeaux Genereux in 1989.

The July Cup has attracted more international stars in recent years, with Agnes World from Japan scoring in 2000, helping the race gain influence on the world stage.

Right
Mick Kinane and the Sir Alex Ferguson owned Rock Of Gibraltar land The Sussex Stakes run at Goodwood racecourse, 2002.

THE SUSSEX STAKES

Group One, three-year-olds and above, one mile

GOODWOOD

The Sussex Stakes is possibly one of the most picturesque Group One races to take place in Britain, and is run on the second day of the five-day Glorious Goodwood Meeting in late-July.

It was founded in 1841, although it was only open to two-year-olds, before 1878, when it was restricted to three-year-olds. The format changed again in 1960 when four-year-olds were allowed to run it and then, in 1975, older horses were finally allowed in.The race is now viewed as the first Group One event of the season which brings together the mixed generations over a mile.

The Sussex Stakes was suspended during both World Wars, and was run at Newmarket in 1941, before returning to Goodwood to become one of the main events in Britain. The race began attracting runners from abroad, with the French sending over four winners from 1960, including Bigstone in 1993. Other notable winners of the event include, Minoru in 1909, My Babu in 1948, Palestine in 1950, Brigadier Gerard in 1971, Bolkonski in 1975, and Rock Of Gibraltar in 2002.

The latter's performance was extra special, as it was his sixth consecutive Group One victory – equalling that of the great Mill Reef – and was the first odds-on winner since 1986. One of the longest priced winners in the race's history was the three-year-old Queen's Hussar at 25-1 in 1963, and it is also that age-group which dominates the Sussex Stakes. Since the race was opened to three-year-olds and above in 1975, 22 of the 31 renewals have fallen to the Classic generation.

THE QUEEN ELIZABETH II STAKES

Group One, three-year-olds and above, one mile

ASCOT

Along with the the King George VI & Queen Elizabeth Stakes, which is also run at Ascot, the Queen Elizabeth II Stakes is one of the newest Group One events, having been founded in 1955. The race was a Group Two affair until being upgraded to Group One status in 1987, and is run on the second day of the three-day Ascot Festival in late-September.

The French were quick to make their mark in the race, winning the first three runnings, before British horses stamped their authority with the great Brigadier Gerard becoming the first winner to defend the title in 1972.

One of the most striking individual performances in the Queen Elizabeth II Stakes took place in 1999, when Dubai

CHAPTER 8

GREAT RACES

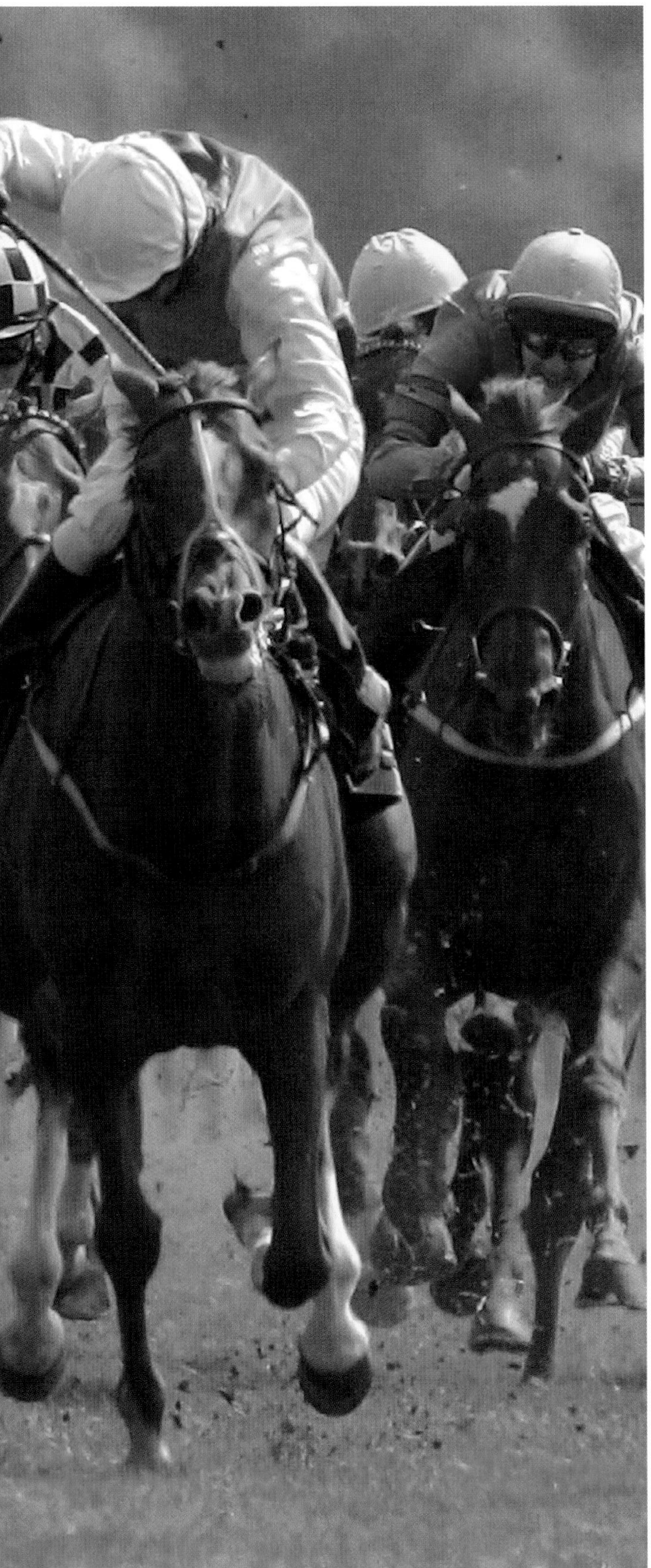

Left
Alan Munro and Sergeant Cecil (black spotted cap) start their run for home to land The Tote Ebor race at York, 2005.

Millennium cantered home on the bridle, and was later hailed by his owner Sheikh Mohammed as the greatest horse he had ever seen. Other popular winners of the race include Rose Bowl in 1975-76, Teleprompter in 1982, Warning in 1988, and Selkirk in 1991.

THE CHAMPION STAKES

Group One, three-year-olds and above, one mile two furlongs

NEWMARKET ROWLEY COURSE

One of the highlights every autumn is the Champion Stakes, staged on the straight Rowley Course at Newmarket, and takes place on the final day of the three-day Champions Meeting in mid-October.

The race was first run in 1877, won by the four-year-old Springfield, before Tristan won the event three times from 1882-84 and in doing so becoming the only treble winner. However, there have been numerous dual winners of the Champion Stakes, with the race also being won by some of the greatest horses in British history.

The following winners all form part of this race's hall of fame: Ormonde in 1886, La Fleche in 1894, Sceptre in 1903, Pretty Polly in 1905, Lemberg in 1910 & 1911, Orpheus in 1920 & 1921, Dynamiter in 1951 & 1952, Sir Ivor in 1968, Triptych in 1986 & 1987, and Alborada in 1998 & 1999.

HANDICAPS

British racing stages some of the most valuable and competitive handicaps in the world, consisting of field-sizes unseen in many countries. In recent years, a series of the most prestigious handicaps have been given the title 'Heritage Handicaps', including the following races:

THE LINCOLN over the straight mile at Doncaster, was founded in 1858, and is run on the final day of the opening three-day meeting of the Flat season in late-March. The race attracted 22 runners with a first prize of £58,000 in 2005, won by Stream Of Gold.

THE CHESTER CUP over two and-a-quarter miles at Chester, was founded in 1858, and is run on the first day of the three-day May Festival at the start of the month. The race attracted 17 runners with a first prize of £69,600 in 2005, won by Anak Pekan.

THE NORTHUMBERLAND PLATE over two miles at Newcastle, was founded in 1833 – formerly known as the Pitmen's Derby – and is run on the second day of the two-day Northumberland meeting in late June. The race attracted 20 runners with a first prize of £104,400 in 2005, won by Sergeant Cecil.

THE JOHN SMITH'S CUP over a mile-and-a-quarter at York, was founded in 1960 – formerly known as the Magnet Cup – and was the first commercially sponsored Flat race in Britain. It is run on the second day of the Cup Meeting in mid-July, and attracted 20 runners with a first prize of £97,500 in 2005, won by Mullins Bay.

THE EBOR over a mile-and-three quarters at York, was founded in 1843, and is run on the second day of the three-day Ebor meeting in mid-August. The race attracted 20 runners with a first prize of £130,000 in 2005, won by Sergeant Cecil.

THE AYR GOLD CUP over six furlongs at Ayr, was founded in 1804, and is run on the final day of the three-day Western Meeting in mid-September. The race attracted 27 runners with a first prize of £70,000 in 2005, won by Presto Shinko.

THE CAMBRIDGESHIRE over one mile one furlong at the Newmarket Rowley Course, was founded in 1839, and is run on the final day of the three-day Cambridgeshire meeting in early October. The race attracted 30 runners with a first prize of £75,400 in 2005, won by Blue Monday.

THE CESAREWITCH over two-and-a-quarter miles at the Newmarket Rowley Course, was founded in 1839, and is run on the final day of the three-day Champions Meeting in mid-October. The race attracted 34 runners with a first prize of £75,400 in 2005, won by the great Sergeant Cecil – who became the first horse to win this race, The Northumberland Plate and The Ebor.

NATIONAL HUNT

THE KING GEORGE VI CHASE

Grade One, four-year-olds and above, three miles
KEMPTON PARK

The second-biggest non-handicap steeplechase event in the National Hunt calendar – only behind the Cheltenham Gold Cup – staged on Boxing Day at Kempton Park.

It was founded in 1937 to commemorate the ascension of King George VI to the throne, and was won by Southern Hero. The race has experienced somewhat of a stop-start journey, with it being suspended in War-time, abandoned due to weather and transferred due to redevelopments at the track.

There have been some memorable winners of the King George VI Chase, including Manicou in 1950 for the Queen Elizabeth, the Queen Mother, and Mill House in 1963. Several horses have also won this race more than once including, Halloween in 1952 & 1954, Mandarin in 1957 & 1959, Pendil in 1972 & 1973, Captain Christy in 1974 & 1975, Silver Buck in 1979 & 1980, The Fellow in 1991 & 1992, One Man in 1995 & 1996, and See More Business in 1997 & 1999.

There has also been a treble winner in Wayward Lad, who took the event in 1982, 1983 & 1985, as well as the great four-times winner Desert Orchid. The popular grey will always be associated with this festive race, after landing his record-breaking fourth success in 1990. Others to set records in this event have been jockey Richard Dunwoody with four victories, and trainers Francois Doumen and Fulke Walwyn, with five each.

Left
Tony McCoy rides Best Mate (left) to victory during the Pertemps King George VI Chase at Kempton Park December 2002.

Left
Charlie Swan celebrates riding Istabraq to win the Smurfit Champion Hurdle Race during the Cheltenham Festival, 2000.

THE CHAMPION HURDLE

Grade One, four-year-olds and above, two miles

CHELTENHAM

The biggest hurdle race to be run during the National Hunt season which, as the name suggests, decides the Champion hurdler of that year. The race is the ultimate examination, usually run at a very fast pace, which not only tests a horse's speed but also their stamina up the final hill.

First run in 1927 for a total prize fund of £365 and won by Blaris, it forms part of the Cheltenham Festival in mid-March, and takes place on the opening day of the four-day bonanza. The Champion Hurdle has seen its share of surprises over the years, with 50-1 outsiders Kirriemuir in 1965, and Beech Road in 1989 catching punters out. However, there have been numerous odds-on winners to sting the bookmakers, with Istabraq being the last in 2000.

The race has seen some fantastic clashes during certain special eras, bringing together a wealth of talent in the same period of time. There was no better example of this than from 1976-81, when Night Nurse, Monksfield, and Sea Pigeon repeatedly locked horns to share the title twice each.

There have been some really notable performances throughout the race's rich history as well, including the five horses to have taken the title on three successive occasions. The first of those was Hatton's Grace from 1949-51, shortly followed by arguably one of the best winners, Sir Ken, who always raised his game at Cheltenham from 1952-54. The next three-times winner came during the period from 1968 to 1970, with Persian War, before See You Then joined the elite list in 1985-87. The final great winner of this event was Istabraq, who raised the roof whenever he came up the hill there, including the year of his third victory in 2000. As with Sir Ken, he was unable to add another title despite a fourth attempt, and it will certainly take a very special horse to re-write the history books.

THE QUEEN MOTHER CHAMPION CHASE

Grade One, five-year-olds and above, two miles

CHELTENHAM

Originally titled the National Hunt Two Mile Champion Chase when founded in 1959 and won by Quita Que, the name was changed in 1980 to commemorate the Queen Mother's 80th birthday. Her Majesty never actually got to win the race itself, but went close with runner-up Game Spirit in 1976, and third-placed Isle of Man in 1977. The race takes place on the second day of the four-day Cheltenham Festival in mid-March, and decides the best two-mile chaser.

The race has been very punter-friendly over the years with Moscow Flyer rewarding favourite backers in 2003 & 2005, while there have only been a few outsiders to take the crown. 1980 saw the biggest priced winner in Another Dolly at 33-1, and a year later Drumgora won at 25-1.

It is quite common to see a horse run in the Queen Mother Champion Chase more than once, as it has become

Right
Desert Orchid (centre) jumping a fence and going on to win the Cheltenham Gold Cup, 1989.

Right inset
Golden Miller with jockey Evan Williams, who rode him to a record fifth consecutive victory in the 1936 Cheltenham Gold Cup.

somewhat of a specialist race bringing together old foes for another round of high speed jumping. There have been several dual winners, including Drinny's Double in 1967-68, Royal Relief in 1972 & 1974, Hilly Way in 1978-79, and Pearlyman in 1987-88. In recent times, there have been another couple of dual winners with Viking Flagship in 1994-95, and Moscow Flyer in 2003 & 2005.

But, it was the performance of the former when landing his first title in 1994 that was one of the best, as he demonstrated his trademark never-say-die attitude in rallying gamely to stick his head out in front and win by just a neck. Neither he nor Moscow Flyer were able to add another crown in later attempts, unlike Badsworth Boy who goes down as one of the greatest winners of the event, after landing it three times between 1983-85.

THE CHELTENHAM GOLD CUP

Grade One, five-year-olds and above, three-and-a-quarter miles

CHELTENHAM

The Cheltenham Gold Cup is simply the most prestigous steeplechase in the National Hunt season, clearly the Blue Riband event. It was first run in 1924 when Red Splash won at 5-1, and takes place on the final day of the four-day Cheltenham Festival. As with many of the Championship races held at the Festival, it is run at a true gallop, testing a horse's ability to jump a fence at speed, as well as having the reserves to make it up the testing hill at the climax of the race.

Prior to 1990, the biggest priced winner of the race was L'Escargot at 33-1 in 1970, but that record was smashed after Norton's Coin surprised everyone at 100-1. Odds-on winners are rarely seen in this event, with the late Best Mate at 8-11 becoming the first since Arkle at 1-10 in 1966.

Both Arkle and Best Mate feature highly on the roll of honour for the Cheltenham Gold Cup, as they both won it three times during the years 1964-66 and 2002-04, respectively, and are joined by another great in Cottage Rake, who dominated in 1948-50.

But one name stands alone when the record books are mentioned, and that is Golden Miller. This great horse won the event a staggering five times between 1932 and 1936, and may have won in 1937 had the race not been abandoned. However, it was the 1935 victory which has gone down as one of the greatest Gold Cup's ever witnessed and Golden Miller's finest.

He came up against Thomond II, who had beaten him at Kempton Park in 1934, and they again went toe-to-toe over the final two fences, before 'The Miller' pulled out extra in claiming his fourth Gold Cup by three-quarters of a length.

There are only a few records which are expected to stand the test of time, and Golden Miller's five Gold Cups is one, as is trainer Michael Dickinson's feat of sending out the first five home in 1983.

WEETABIX
National Westminster
National meeting

Left
Red Rum in his last Grand National win, 1977.

THE GRAND NATIONAL

Grade Three, six-year-olds and above, four-and-a-half miles

AINTREE

Founded in 1839, the Grand National is one of the most famous races in the world.

The idea for it came from William Lynn, a local hotel owner, and the inaugural running was won by Lottery, the 5-1 favourite. Although the 1839 Grand National was the first 'official' running, the race had taken place for three years beforehand, with the 1836 version going to The Duke, ridden by Captain Becher, who had a fence named after him following his fall at the obstacle in 1839.

The fences employed during the early years were completely different from those of today, with hedges and stone walls before the introduction of the more familiar fences known to so many today as Valentines Brook, the Chair, Becher's Brook, the Canal Turn and the Water Jump, making a total of 30 fences in all.

The race was moved south to a site at Gatwick during the First World War, before being cancelled for four years during the Second World War. During the sixties the Grand National lost some its glamour, with uncertainty as to whether Aintree was to be sold, and then in the seventies attendances hit and all-time low. The race then bounced back with the aid of sponsorship, along with the high-profile three-times winner Red Rum. It was also his third victory in 1977 which stands firm as one of the most memorable races, as he destroyed the other 41 runners to win by an amazing 25 lengths. No other horse has yet to win the race twice since 1977, let alone three times.

Other notable races from the Grand National's long history include, the dual-winner Manifesto running in his eighth National in 1904, Foinavon becoming the biggest priced winner at 100-1 after avoiding a huge pile-up at the twenty-third fence, Poethlyn winning his second National to become the shortest priced winner in the process at 11-4, Jenny Pitman being the first woman to train the winner with Corbiere in 1983 before following up with Royal Athlete in 1995, and trainer Ginger McCain joining Fred Rimell on four wins apiece in 2004 after Amberleigh House won from the same stable as Red Rum.

OTHER RACES & HANDICAPS

THE BETFAIR LANCASHIRE CHASE over three miles at Haydock, founded only in 2005, and is run in mid-November near the start of the National Hunt season. The inaugural running attracted seven runners with a first prize of £85,530, won by Kingscliff. The race was introduced as part of a three-race series including the King George VI Chase and the Cheltenham Cup, with a prize of £1 million going to the winner of all three races in the same season.

THE TINGLE CREEK CHASE over two miles at Sandown Park, was previously run as the The Sandown

Right
Coombe Hill ridden by Jamie Osborne (centre) on his way to victory in the Hennessy Cognac Gold Cup at Newbury, 1996.

Far right
Legendary TV commentator Sir Peter O'Sullivan relaxes on his last day for the BBC during the Hennessy Gold Cup at Newbury in 1997.

Pattern Chase until 1979, when it was renamed after the great racehorse Tingle Creek. The race is run on the second day of the two-day Tingle Creek Meeting at the start of December and attracted seven runners with a first prize of £71,275 in 2005, won by Kauto Star.

THE HENNESSY GOLD CUP over three miles-and-a-quarter at Newbury, was founded in 1957 – held at Cheltenham before switching to Newbury in 1960 – and is run on the second day of the three-day Hennessy Meeting in late-November. The race attracted 19 runners with a first prize of £71,275 in 2005, won by Trabolgan.

THE BETFRED (WHITBREAD) GOLD CUP over three miles five furlongs, was founded in 1957, and is run on the final weekend of the National Hunt season in late April. The race attracted 19 runners with a first prize of £87,000 in 2005, won by Jack High.

IRELAND

FLAT

THE IRISH TWO THOUSAND GUINEAS

Group One, three-year-old colts and fillies, one mile
CURRAGH

Founded in 1921, and won by Soldennis, the Irish Two Thousand Guineas, is traditionally run about three weeks after the English equivalent in late May. The Irish version often attracts the winner of that race, but the feat of winning both is rare with only the following horses managing it: Right Tack in 1969, Don't Forget Me in 1987, Tirol in 1990, Rodrigo De Triano in 1993, and Rock Of Gibraltar in 2002.

The trainers O'Brien have a good record in the race, although not related, with Vincent training five winners, and Aidan, four, in recent times. There was also another victory for Vincent's son David in 1985 with Triptych.

Other notable winners of the race include Baytown in 1928, Santa Claus in 1964, Sadler's Wells in 1984, and Spinning World in 1996 who thus became the first success for the French.

THE IRISH ONE THOUSAND GUINEAS

Group One, three-year-old fillies, one mile
CURRAGH

The female version of the Guineas was first run a year after the male equivalent in 1922, and was won by Lady Violette. The pattern of running the One Thousand Guineas after the Two Thousand Guineas

has continued, with the race these days taking place on a Sunday in late-May.

Unlike the Two Thousand Guineas, winners of the English One Thousand Guineas have struggled to add the Irish version. That was until 2004 when Attraction made history. Mark Johnston's filly succeeded where the other eight Newmarket winners failed, crossing the Irish Sea to get home by a length.

The trainers O'Brien have also done well in this event, winning three a piece, while the French have had more success than with the male version, with Alec Head sending out three winners from 1956-59.

There were some notable winners of the race during the nineties, including the following talented fillies: In The Groove in 1990, Kooyonga in 1991, Marling in 1992, and Ridgewood Pearl in 1995.

Left
Mick Kinane and Galileo return to the winners enclosure after powering to an easy victory in the Budweiser Irish Derby, 2001.

THE IRISH DERBY

Group One, three-year-old colts and fillies, one mile four furlongs

CURRAGH

The Irish Derby was founded in 1866, when Selim was the first winner. The horse incredibly won on each day of the meeting that year, then staged over four days. The first six runnings of the race were over a mile-and-three-quarters, but in 1872 it was altered to its current distance of a mile-and-a-half.

The Irish Derby has become one of the prestige events in Europe in recent times, attracting the Derby winners from England and France. It is run on the final day of the three-day Derby meeting in early-July, and has become more popular since the introduction of level weights in 1946, including an allowance for fillies.

The first English Derby winner to run in the Irish Derby was Orby in 1907 and he succeeded, a feat which has been repeated by the following great horses, reading as a who's who of British Flat racing in the modern era: Santa Claus in 1964, Nijinsky in 1970, Grundy in 1975, The Minstrel in 1977, Shirley Heights in 1978, Troy in 1979, Shergar in 1982, Shahrastani in 1986, Kahyasi in 1988, Generous in 1991, Commander In Chief in 1993, Sinndar in 2000, Galileo in 2001, and High Chaparral in 2002.

Once again, Vincent O'Brien features prominently on the roll of honour, having won the race six times, and he was responsible for three of the above horses – Nijinsky, The Minstrel, and El Gran Senor. There have also been four French Derby winners to complete the double, with Montjeu being the last in 1999.

The Irish Derby usually works out as the formbook suggests and shocks are rare. The longest priced winner was Zarathustra at 50-1 in 1954, and the last odds-on shot came in 2005, when Hurricane Run won at 4-5.

THE IRISH OAKS

Group One, three-year-old fillies, one mile four furlongs

CURRAGH

The Irish Oaks was founded 29 years after the Irish Derby in 1895, was first won by Sapling, and is run a few weeks after the male version on the second day of the two-day Oaks Meeting in mid-July.

As with the Irish Derby, there is a rich history of English Oaks winners crossing the sea in an attempt to record the double, with nine fillies managing the great feat. The first of those was Masaka in 1948, along with the following: Altesse Royale in 1971, Juliette Marny in 1975, Unite in 1987, User Friendly in 1992, Ramruma in 1999 and Ouija Board in 2004.

There have been a number of fillies who have failed in their attempt at the Oaks double, including Mysterious in 1973, who was thrashed by the French-trained Dahlia, one of the greatest winners of the Irish Oaks. Sir Michael Stoute stands out as the

Right
Jim Culloty and Timbera (7) land The Powers Gold Label Irish Grand National Steeple Chase Race run at Fairyhouse, 2003.

leading trainer of the event with five winners, the last of those coming in 2000 with Petrushka.

THE IRISH ST. LEGER

Group One, three-year-olds and above, one mile six furlongs

CURRAGH

Unlike the English equivalent, the Irish St. Leger, founded in 1915 and won by La Poloma, allows older horses to run as well as the Classic generation.

The race is currently run just one week after the St. Leger at Doncaster, with horses attempting the double finding it more elusive than in the Derby and Oaks, with only three accomplishing such an achievement. The first to succeed, was Royal Lancer in 1922, then came Trigo in 1929, before Touching Wood in 1982.

Until 1994 there had been no dual winner of the race, but Vintage Crop became the first when following up his 1993 victory. Ironically, two horses managed to match that immediately afterwards when Oscar Schindler won in 1996-97, and Kayf Tara the following two years.

Vincent O'Brien again features proudly as the greatest trainer of this Classic with a staggering nine victories, starting with Barclay in 1959, and finishing with Dark Lomond in 1988. The leading jockey was Tommy Burns, with six victories, as well as training Vimadee to win in 1961.

NATIONAL HUNT

THE IRISH GRAND NATIONAL

Grade A, five-year-olds and above, three miles five furlongs

FAIRYHOUSE

Founded in 1870, and run on the second day of the three-day Easter Festival in mid-April, the Irish Grand National – along with the racecourse – has grown in stature since then.

The race was dominated in the sixties and seventies by the Dreapers. Tom Dreaper had already won it three times, before a run of seven successive victories, starting in 1960 with Olympia, and followed by Fortria in 1961, Kerforo in 1962, Last Link in 1963, Arkle in 1964, Splash in 1965 and finally Flyingbolt in 1966. It was then son Jim's turn, winning it four times over the next five years.

There have been some notable performances in the race, including the afore-mentioned Tom Dreaper's seventh successive victory, coming courtesy of Flyingbolt under 12st 7lbs on a day when the trainer won five other races on the same card!

The Irish Grand National can these days be used as a guide to the English Grand National the following year, with Bobbyjo completing the double in 1998-99, before Numbersixvalverde became the latest winner to march onto Aintree glory in 2006 after winning at Fairyhouse in 2005.

There are two other major Grand Nationals which take place on the British racing calendar, with the first of them coming over the Festive period at Chepstow.

The Welsh National is run over three miles five furlongs, usually on very heavy ground, and attracted 18 runners for a first prize of £57,020 in 2005, won by L'Aventure.

The Scottish Grand National over four miles one furlong, has been run at Ayr since 1966, following the closure of Bogside, and is traditionally run a few weeks after Aintree in late-April. The race attracted 20 runners with a first prize of £70,000 in 2005 and was won by Joes Edge.

REST OF THE WORLD

FRANCE

THE GRAND PRIX DU JOCKEY CLUB over a mile-and-a-quarter at Chantilly for three-year-old colts and fillies, was founded in 1836, and is run in early-June. The race attracted 17 runners for a first prize of £607,872 in 2005, won by Shamardal. Other notable recent winners of the event include, Caerleon in 1983, Bering in 1986, Old Vic in 1989, Peintre Celebre in 1997, Montjeu in 1999, and Sulamani in 2002.

The owner with the most victories was Marcel Boussac, who won it 12 times from 1922-78, while trainer Tom Jennings had ten triumphs from 1852-1882, and Yves Saint-Martin, the top jockey, with nine between 1965-87.

THE GRAND PRIX DE PARIS over a mile-and-a-half at Longchamp for three-year-old colts and fillies, was founded in 1863, and is now run in mid-July. The time and distance of the race has been altered over the years, and attracted nine runners for a first prize of £202,624 in 2005, won by Scorpion. Other notable recent winners include, Glint Of Gold for trainer Ian Balding in 1981, At Talaq in 1984 who later secured the Melbourne Cup, and Bago in 2004, who went on to land the Prix de l'Arc De Triomphe. The owner with the most victories was Edmond Blanc, winning seven times between 1879-1904, while trainer Francois Mathet had nine winners from 1953-82, and Tom Lane, the top jockey with six between 1888-99.

THE PRIX DE L'ABBAYE over five furlongs at Longchamp for juveniles and above, was founded in 1957 to commemorate the hundredth anniversary of the racecourse and is run earlier on during the Prix de l'Arc De Triomphe card. The race attracted 17 runners for a first prize of £81,050 in 2005, won by Avonbridge, who was yet another British-trained winner of this prestigous sprint.

The British raiders hold a superb record in this event, Be Friendly becoming the first in 1968 and followed by the likes of, Moorestyle in 1980, Sharpo in 1982, Habibti in 1983, Committed in 1984 & 1985, Keen Hunter in 1991, Mr Brooks in 1992, Carmine Lake in 1997, and Patavellian in 2003 to name but a few.

7
POWERS
GOLD

Below
Pat Eddery of Ireland holds the plate aloft after his victory on Dancing Brave in the Prix de L'Arc de Triomphe at Longchamp, 1986.

Below right
Sinndar winning the 2000 Prix de L'Arc de Triomphe for Ireland.

Two winners missing from that list were arguably the best of the bunch, namely, Dayjur, who destroyed his rivals in 1990, and the filly Lochsong, who became a dual winner in 1993 & 1994.

The late Sir Robert Sangster enjoyed no less than four successes in the 'Abbaye', while trainer Francois Mathet had eight winners between 1957-74, and Yves Saint-Martin rode five between 1962-74.

THE PRIX DE L'ARC DE TRIOMPHE over a mile-and-a-half for three-year-olds and above, was founded in 1920, won by Comrade, and is run on the first Sunday of October. The race attracted 15 winners for a first prize of £729,447 in 2005, won by Hurricane Run.

There have been six dual winners of the 'Arc', with Ksar becoming the first in 1921 & 1922, followed by Motrico in 1930 & 1932, Corrida in 1936 & 1937, Tantieme in 1950 & 1951, Ribot 1955 & 1956, and finally Alleged in 1977 & 1978. There have been some superb winners to enter this highly prestigous hall of fame including the likes of Brantome in 1934, Caracalla in 1946, Ballymoss in 1958, Sea Bird II in 1965, Mill Reef in 1971, Allez France in 1974, Dancing Brave in 1986, Lammtarra in 1995, Montjeu in 1999, and Sinndar in 2000.

Marcel Boussac owned no fewer than six winners of the 'Arc', while leading trainer Andre Fabre currently sits on six winners – the first coming courtesy of Trempolino in 1987 – with Hurricane Run being his very recent last in 2005.

THE GRAND STEEPLE CHASE DE PARIS over three miles five furlongs, was founded in 1874, and is run towards the end of May at Auteuil. The race attracted 18 runners for a first prize of £191,489 in 2005, won by Sleeping Jack.

The figure-of-eight racecourse is one of the most unique in the world, asking horses to run in both directions through brush fences – rather than over them. The nature of the event has seen little success from British raiders, with the brave Mandarin

being the last winner in 1962, a courageous effort considering he jumped the last twenty fences without the bit in his mouth.

Trainer Francois Doumen has enjoyed five victories in the race, with the likes of The Fellow and First Gold.

ITALY

THE DERBY ITALIANO over a mile-and-half for three-year-old colts and fillies, was founded in 1884 – won by Andreina – and is run towards the end of May at Capannelle, Rome. The race attracted 15 runners for a first prize of £331,915 in 2005, won by De Sica, after the prize-money was given a significant boost in 2001.

The event was passed around racecourses during the early years, until finding a permanent home at Capannelle in 1926 – although it was again briefly run at San Siro during the mid-1940's. Since the race was opened up to non-Italian bred horses in 1981, British runners have fared well, and they feature among this list of notable winners such as, Nearco in 1938, Orange Bay in 1975, Glint Of Gold in 1981, White Muzzle in 1993, Luso in 1995, Central Park in 1998, and Rakti in 2002.

Four British trainers have also won the race twice each, including, Clive Brittain in 1991 & 1995, Peter Chapple-Hyam in 1993 & 1997, Paul Cole in 1987 & 1994, and Michael Jarvis in 1989 & 2001.

GERMANY

THE DEUTSCHES DERBY over a mile-and-a-half for three-year-old colts and fillies, was founded in 1869 – won by Investment – and is run in early-July at Hamburg. The race attracted 12 runners for a first prize of £214,894 in 2005, won by Nicaron.

The race was firstly given the title of Norddeutsches Derby, before adopting its current name in 1889, with it being run at Hoppegarten and Munich during the Second World War.

The race has been mainly dominated by home-trained horses, and one of the greatest winners was Acatenango in 1985, who also added over a dozen more events throughout Europe.

The leading owner in the race was Gestut Schlenderhan, with sixteen victories from 1908-76, while the top trainer was George Arnull with nine successes, and top jockey was Gerhard Streit with eight triumphs.

THE GROSSER PREIS VON BADEN over a mile-and-a-half for three-year-olds and above, was founded in 1858, and is run in early-September at Baden Baden. The race attracted nine runners for a first prize of £319,150 in 2005 – the richest race in Germany – and was won by the British-trained Warrsan.

There have been no less than three dual winners of this event, including Marduk in 1974 & 1975, Mondrian in 1989 & 1990, and Tiger Hill in 1998 & 1999, although, Kincsem won it three times consecutively back in 1877-79.

The leading trainers in recent times, with five victories each include, Sven von Mitzlaff between 1962-73, Heinz Jentzsch from 1970-94, and Harry Wragg during 1963-81.

CZECH REPUBLIC

THE VELKA PARDUBICKA over four-and-a-quarter miles, was founded in 1874 – won by Fantome – and is run on the second Sunday in October at Pardubice racecourse. The race attracted 18 runners for a first prize of £52,484 in 2005, won by Maskul.

This unique race draws parallels with the Grand National at Aintree, providing the sternest of tests for any European steeplechaser. The course includes some very hazardous obstacles such as the following fences:

Fence two – boasts a very wide hedge with a ditch.

Fence four – the biggest on the course, and has been responsible for the demise of up to a third of the runners at the same time.

Fence six – the 'Popkovices Turn', on a bend with a ditch, causing ten fallers in 1998

Fences eight & nine – two rapid hedges that come close together.

Fence fourteen – the 'Poplars Jump', which includes a small set of timber rails.

Fence fifteen – the 'Drop', where many horses unseat their riders.

Fence sixteen – featuring a stone wall.

Fence eighteen – the largest of the water jumps, which has been reduced in recent years due to some bad falls.

Fence twenty-two – the 'Dry Ditch', which catches many out, as there is no fence, just a deep ditch to be cleared.

Fence twenty-five – the 'English Jump', similar to the Chair at Aintree, but with an even higher landing side.

The nature of the test has three-times seen just one horse come home in isolation in 1899, 1920 and 1993, whereas in 1909 no horse even managed to complete the course. The most successful horse in the history of the event was four-times winner Zeleznik from 1987-91, who was saddled by the leading jockey, the courageous Josef Vana, with five triumphs from 1987-1997. The first post-war British winner was Stephens Society in 1973, and It's A Snip became the second in 1995.

DUBAI

THE DUBAI WORLD CUP over a mile-and-a-quarter boasts the title of being the richest horse race in the world.

Founded in 1996 – won by the American-trained Cigar – it is run on the prestige World Cup Day, featuring a host of other Group One events, at Nad al Sheba in Dubai during late-March. The race is held on a dirt surface, and attracted 11 runners for a colossal first prize of £2,093,023 in 2006, won by Electrocusionist.

In its brief history, the race has been won by some real superstars, including Cigar, followed by the likes of Singspiel in 1997, Silver Charm in 1998, Almutawakel in 1999, Dubai Millennium in 2000, Roses In May in 2005, and Electrocusionist in 2006, with the latter taking Godolphin well clear of the owner's leaderboard on five victories.

UNITED STATES OF AMERICA

THE KENTUCKY DERBY over a mile-and-a-quarter, was founded in 1875 – won by Aristides – and is run on the first Saturday in May at Churchill Downs racetrack, forming the first-leg of the US Triple Crown. The race, is also referred to as the 'Run for the Roses', as flowers have been presented to the winning jockey from 1896, the same year in which the distance was reduced from its original mile-and-a-half. The 2005 running attracted 20 runners for a first prize of £853,958, and was won by Giacomo.

Amongst the most notable winners of this event are, War Admiral in 1939, Citation in 1948, Northern Dancer in 1964, Secretariat in 1973, Seattle Slew in 1977, Affirmed in 1978, Sunday Silence in 1989, Thunder Gulch in 1995, Silver Charm in 1997, Fusaichi Pegasus in 2000, War Emblem in 2002, and Smarty Jones in 2004.

Heading the owners leaderboard is Calumet Farm with eight victories, where as two individuals share the leading jockeys tally – Eddie Arcaro and Bill Hartack – with five each.

THE PREAKNESS STAKES over one mile one-and-half furlong on dirt , was founded in 1873 – won by Survivor – and is run about three weeks after the Kentucky Derby at Pimlico racetrack, forming the second-leg of the US Triple Crown. The race attracted 14 runners for a first prize of £338,542 in 2005, won by Afleet Alex.

Both the venue and the distance of this event were changed during the early days, before finding a regular home at Pimlico, where it has been run since.

Amongst the most notable winners of the Preakness are, Man O'War in 1920, War Admiral in 1937, Whirlaway in 1941, Citation in 1948, Native Dancer in 1953, Northern Dancer in

Left
Singspiel ridden by Jerry Baily wins the Dubai World Cup, 1997.

Right
Arazi ridden by Pat Valenzuela storms to a brilliant victory at the 1991 Breeders' Cup.

1964, Secretariat in 1973, Seattle Slew in 1977, Affirmed in 1978, Silver Charm in 1997, War Emblem in 2002, and Smarty Jones in 2004.

Calumet Farm once again heads the top of the owners table for the Preakness, this time with seven victories between 1941-68, while trainer Robert Wyndham Walden recorded seven wins between 1875-88, and Eddie Acaro stands as the leading jockey with five triumphs, the first coming in 1948.

THE BELMONT STAKES over a mile-and-a-half on dirt, was founded in 1867 – won by Ruthless – and is run in mid-June at Belmont Park, New York, as the final-leg of the US Triple Crown. It is the oldest of all three races, and arguably the most important as horses attempt to win here in order to enter the history books. In all, there have been 29 attempts at the Triple Crown, with only 11 proving good enough on the big day at Belmont. The talented 11 to make the elite list are: **1919 Sir Barton, 1930 Gallant Fox, 1935 Omaha, 1937 War Admiral, 1941 Whirlaway, 1943 Count Fleet, 1946 Assault, 1948 Citation, 1973 Secretariat, 1977 Seattle Slew, 1978 Affirmed.**

In 2005 the event – named after the first President of the American Jockey Club August Belmont – attracted 11 runners for a first prize of £312,500 in 2005, won by Afleet Alex.

The race was moved to its current home Belmont Park in 1904 – although it was transferred due to redevelopment during 1963-67 – and two years later, the distance was finally set at a mile-and-a-half after fluctuating from one mile five furlongs to nine furlongs. The event was also cancelled from 1911-12 owing to an anti-betting law in New York.

Three owners share the spoils with six wins each in the Belmont, including, James R Keene from 1879-1910, Belair Stud between 1930-55, and the Belmont Family from 1869-1983. James Rowe heads the leading trainers list with eight successes from 1883-1913, while Eddie Acaro from 1941-55 and James McLaughlin between 1882-88 share the jockey's spoils with six each.

THE ARLINGTON MILLION over a mile-and-a-quarter on turf for three-year-olds and above, was only founded in 1981 – won by John Henry – and is run during mid-August at Arlington Park, near Chicago. It attracted ten runners for a first prize of £312,500 in 2005, won by the British-trained Powerscourt.

The race earnt its name for being the first ever million dollar event for thoroughbreds, before being temporarily transferred to Woodbine in Canada for the 1988 renewal, and cancelled from 1998-99, as Arlington racetrack was closed.

One of the most memorable races took place in 1984, when the inaugural winner, John Henry – also finished runner-up in 1983 – came back to triumph again aged nine-years-old, an age not associated with top Flat race-winners around the world. There have been some other notable performances since, including, Teleprompter in 1985, Estrapade in 1986, Manila in 1987, Steinlen in 1989, Tight Spot in 1991, Awad in 1995, and Beat Hollow in 2002.

THE BREEDERS' CUP was founded in 1984 at Hollywood Park, a concept that was designed towards becoming the equine version of the Olympics, bringing together the best thoroughbreds across the globe. As with the Olympics, the meeting takes place at a different venue each time – every year in late October/early-November – and consists of eight Grade One Championship events.

The event has been staged at the following racetracks:

Churchill Downs – a record five times in 1988, 1991, 1994, 1998, 2000, and scheduled for 2006
Belmont Park – four times in 1990, 1995, 2001 & 2005
Gulfstream Park – three times in 1989, 1992 & 1999
Hollywood Park – three times in 1984, 1987 & 1997
Santa Anita – three times in 1986, 1993 & 2003
Aqueduct – once in 1985
Arlington Park – once in 2002
Lone Star Park – once in 2004

The eight races which form the Breeders' Cup, the world's second richest meeting behind the Dubai World Cup, are as follows:

Juvenile Fillies over one mile for two-year-old fillies
2005 – First prize of £287,083 – won by Folklore
Juvenile over one mile for two-year-olds
2005 – First prize of £406,250 – won by Stevie Wonderboy
Filly & Mare Turf over a mile-and-a-quarter for three-year-olds and above
2005 – First prize of £287,083 – won by Intercontinental
Sprint over six furlongs for three-year-olds and above
2005 – First prize of £287,083 – won by Silver Train
Mile Turf over a mile for three-year-olds and above
2005 – First prize of £548,438 – won by Artie Schiller
Distaff over one mile one furlong for three-year-olds and above
2005 – First prize of £541,667 – won by Pleasant Home
Breeders' Cup Turf over a mile-and-a-half for three-year-olds and above
2005 – First prize of £617,500 – won by Shirocco
Breeders' Cup Classic over a mile-and-a-quarter for three-year-olds and above
2005 – First prize of £1,267,500 – won by Saint Liam

The leading owner at the Breeders' Cup is Allen E.Paulson with six victories, while the top trainer is D.Wayne Lukas with a sensational 17 triumphs, nine clear of his nearest rival. The leading jockey is Jerry Bailey with 14 wins.

There have been many memorable races and winners throughout the history of this fantastic spectacle, but the one which stands out for many is that of Arazi. There is no better sight in horseracing than that of a horse cutting through the entire field of runners cruising, without being put under any pressure – a very rare sign of class. But in 1991, during the Juvenile for colts, Arazi recorded such a feat, coming effortlessly from last to first, bounding further and further away up the straight to stretch his unbeaten record to seven.

Right
Makybe Diva ridden by Glen Boss wins the Tooheys New Melbourne Cup in 2003.

British raiders have enjoyed their share of glory, with the following notable winners, Pebbles in the 1985 Turf, Royal Academy in the 1990 Turf, Sheikh Albadou in the 1991 Turf, Barathea in 1994, Ridgewood Pearl in 1995, Pilsudski in the 1996 Turf, Daylami in the 1999 Turf, Kalanisi in the 2000 Turf, High Chaparral in the 2002 & 2003 Turf, Islington in the 2003 Filly & Mare Turf, and Ouija Board in the 2004 Filly & Mare Turf.

CANADA

THE CANADIAN INTERNATIONAL over a mile-and-a-half on turf was founded in 1938 – won by Bunty Lawless – and is run in late-October at Woodbine racetrack, Toronto. The race attracted ten runners in 2005, for a first prize of £521,739, won by Relaxed Gesture.

The race was originally named the Long Branch Championship, run on dirt at Long Branch racetrack, and was run at a distance just over a mile. The conditions then altered over the next few decades, before 1956, when the race moved to Woodbine, and then two years later, was run on turf for the first time. It was not until 1987, however, that the distance changed to its current format of a mile-and-a-half.

The Canadian International has become one of the biggest events in the world for middle-distance horses, and has been won in the past by the following: Secretariat in 1973, Dahlia in 1974, Snow Knight in 1975, Majesty's Prince in 1982 & 1984, Snurge in 1992, Singspiel in 1996, Mutafaweq in 2000, Mutamam in 2001, Phoenix Reach in 2003, and Sulamani in 2004.

AUSTRALIA

THE CAULFIELD CUP over a mile-and-a-half on turf was founded in 1879 – won by Newminster – and takes place in mid-October at Flemington racetrack, Melbourne. The race attracted 18 runners for a first prize of £618,367 in 2005, won by Railings. The Caulfield Cup is one of the leading handicaps to be run

in Australia, and is often used as a useful trial for the prestige Melbourne Cup, run later in November.

Paris was the first dual winner of this event in 1892 & 1894, and since then, the following horses have all won the race twice: Hymettus in 1898 & 1991, Poseidon in 1906 & 1907, Uncle Sam in 1912 & 1914, Whittier in 1922 & 1925, Rising Fast in 1954 & 1955, and Ming Dynasty in 1977 & 1980.

THE COX PLATE over a mile-and-a-quarter on turf was founded in 1922 – won by Violencello – and is run in mid-October at Moonee Valley racetrack, Victoria. The race is the second-richest event in Australia – behind the Melbourne Cup – and was named after the founder of the racetrack – William Samuel Cox. The race attracted 14 runners for a first prize £744,898 in 2005, won by Makybe Diva.

Amongst the previous winners of the Cox Plate are, Phar Lap in 1930 & 1931, Rising Fast in 1954, Kingston Town in 1980, 1981 & 1982, Octagonal in 1995, Might And Power in 1998, Northerly in 2001 & 2002, and the great Maykbe Diva in 2005.

THE MELBOURNE CUP over two miles was founded in 1861 – won by Archer for a first prize of £710 along with a gold watch – and is run on the first Tuesday of November at Flemington racetrack, Melbourne. The race attracted 24 runners for a first prize of £1,265,306 in 2005, won by Makybe Diva. The event is not only the biggest in Australia, but also one of the most prestigious in the world, and is famously referred to as 'the race that stops the nation'.

The race did not take long in attracting huge crowds, as by the 1880s, attendances for Melbourne Cup Day had reached 100,000. There were 106,479 present for the 2005 renewal. The activity away from the track gets as much attention as the race itself, with a similar atmosphere to that of 'Ladies Day' at Royal Ascot, seeing awards being presented for best-dressed race goers.

The Melbourne Cup trophy itself has changed over the years, having been a silver and rose bowl, as well as a gold and silver horse figurine, until 1919 when the current Gold Cup model was presented.

There have been few shocks in the race in recent years, but there have been three 100-1 shots to take the Cup, with The Pearl in 1871, Wotan in 1936, and Old Rowley in 1940. The shortest-priced winner, however, was the only ever odds-on shot, and that was the great Phar Lap in 1930 at odds of 8-11. Phar Lap was also one of the greatest winners of the Melbourne Cup, ranking alongside two other winners of this race in Carbine and Makybe Diva. The former won 33 of his 43 races – including a staggering four times on the same day – and took the 1890 renewal by carrying a record ten stone five pounds, against a record 38 runners, in a record time. The latter is arguably the greatest winner of the event, when becoming the first three-times winner in 2003, 2004 & 2005.

The leading trainer of the Melbourne Cup is Bart Cummings, with 11 victories from 1965-99, while Irish trainer, Dermot Weld, became the first European handler with Vintage Crop in 1993, before following up with Media Puzzle in 2002.

JAPAN

THE JAPAN CUP over a mile-and-a-half on turf was founded in 1981 – won by Mairzy Doates – and is run on the last Sunday of November at Tokyo racetrack. The race attracted 18 runners for a first prize of £1,290,418 in 2005, won by Alkaased. There is also another version run on dirt the day before, over a mile-and-a-quarter.

In its brief history, the Japan Cup has quickly established itself as one of the leading events in the world for middle-distance horses on turf, with winners coming from all across the globe, including the likes of: Jupiter Island from Great Britain in 1986, Le Glorieux from France in 1987, Horlicks from New Zealand in 1989, Better Loosen Up from Australia in 1989, Lando from Germany in 1995, Singspiel (GB) in 1996, Pilsudski (GB) in 1997, El Condor Pasa from Japan in 1998, Falbrav from Italy in 2002, and Zenno Rob Roy (JPN) in 2004.

HONG KONG

THE HONG KONG CUP over a mile-and-a-quarter on turf was founded in 1988 – won by Flying Dancer – and is run in mid-December at Sha Tin racetrack. The race attracted ten runners for a first prize of £683,646 in 2005, won by Vengeance Of Rain.

The distance of the event was run over one mile one furlong until 1999, the same year it was also handed Group One status, which has helped the race grow in stature. As with the Japan Cup, the race is contested by horses from across the world, and has been won by the likes of, State Taj from Australia in 1994, Fujiyama Kenzan from Japan in 1995, First Island from Great Britain in 1996, Val's Prince from the United States in 1997, Jim And Tonic from France in 1999, and Alexander Goldrun from Ireland in 2004.

Below
Canadian-bred Northern Dancer.

Below right
Derrick Smith of The Coolmore breeding operation at Newmarket, 2006.

Far right
A horse goes through the sales ring during the sales held at Doncaster.

CHAPTER 9
BREEDING

The breeding of horses has existed since the year dot, but the concept of the modern thoroughbred racehorse originated in the mid-17th century, when Arabian stallions were imported to breed with English mares. There were three Arabian stallions in particular – the Foundation Sires – whose genes can be traced through to every modern racehorse today, namely, the Byerley Turk (born approximately in 1680), the Darley Arabian (1700), and the Godolphin Arabian (1724).

During this period the first breeders emerged, with James D'Arcy amongst them. Charles II employed D'Arcy as Master of the Royal Stud in 1660 at Tutbury Castle, Staffordshire, which was first established by Henry VIII. His role was to breed His Majesty's colts after horse numbers in England had declined following the Civil War, and was to be a significant moment in the history of breeding.

Just over one hundred years later, one of the first leading sires in Britain emerged, Eclipse (1764-1789) who after an unbeaten career on the track, went on to produce well over three hundred foals. It is said that up to 90 per cent of all modern-day thoroughbreds can be traced back to this great horse.

It was not until centuries later, however, that a new type of owner-breeder emerged.

From the turn of the 20th century through to the Second World War, owner-breeders such as Lord Derby and the Aga Khan III flexed their financial muscle, mopping up the leading breeders titles on no fewer than 18 occasions between them, along with numerous English Classics.

It was also around this period when another of the greatest modern-day sires appeared. This was the Canadian-bred Northern Dancer (1961-1990) who after winning the Kentucky Derby and Preakness Stakes became the leading thoroughbred sire of all-time. During his illustrious career at stud, he produced a mammoth 146 stakes winners, including Nijinksy, The Minstrel and El Gran Senor. He was also the proud parent of Sadler's Wells. Such was the demand for stock of Northern Dancer that at the Keeneland Sales in 1993 one of his colts, Snaafi Dancer, became the first yearling to be sold at auction for $10 million.

The trend for wealthy investors continued over the following decades, with the likes of Robert Sangster founding the Coolmore Stud. Sangster also produced Sadler's Wells, who went on to become the leading sire in Britain on 15 occasions in 16 years from 1990, helping the Coolmore Stud to become one of the most powerful in the world, along with the likes of the Godolphin satellite operation in Dubai and England.

The world of breeding is now a multi-million pound industry, with stallions changing hands for vast sums before

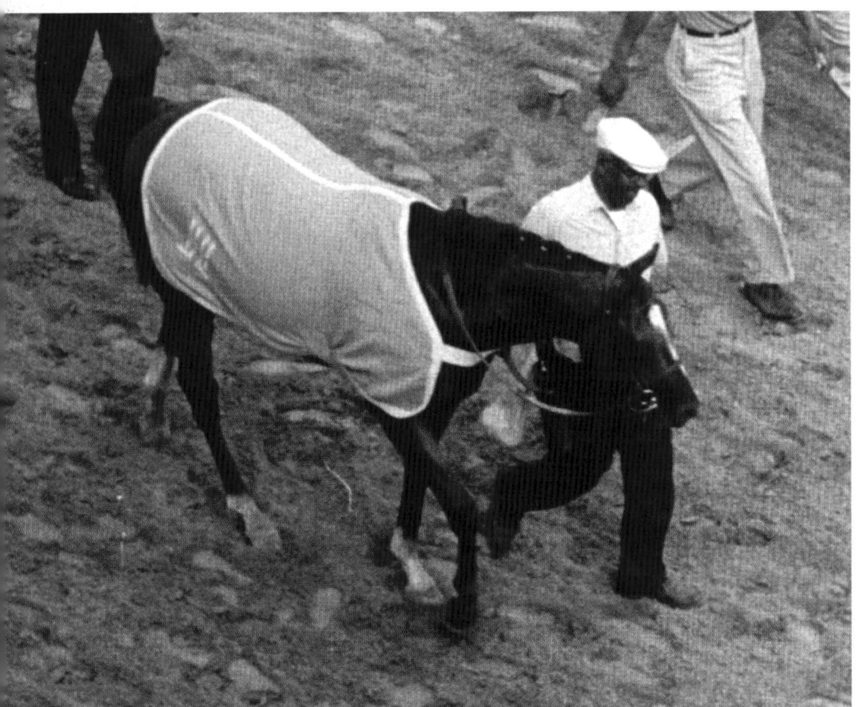

standing at stud. The stallions and mares become the stars of the equine world when stabled, receiving luxurious treatment, down to the smallest of detail. The pastures on which they spend many an hour are kept insect-free, as are their five-star stables, whilst they are fed on the best oats and bran. There are hundreds of these studs spread across the globe, with the following amongst the biggest in the British Isles:

COOLMORE, Ireland – the biggest breeding operation in the world, with studs in American and Australia, and a history stretching back over 50 years.

CHEVELEY PARK STUD, England – one of the most successful farms in Europe, located in Newmarket, with over 1,000 acres of land.

DARLEY STUD, England – Stood 48 stallions in eight countries during 2005, including America, Australia, Dubai, Europe, and Japan.

JUDDMONTE FARMS, England – has no fewer than nine farms in England, Ireland and America, and has produced well over a hundred Group One winners.

In the United States of America, Kentucky is the main breeding state, with almost 40 studs, and along with Florida and California, makes the largest contribution towards the 35,000 thoroughbred foals registered in the country each year.

The next phase in the cycle of the breeding operation is to send the foals to auction, and the following sales rings are amongst the biggest in the British Isles:

DONCASTER, England – founded in 1962, is Britain's second biggest bloodstock auctioneers. It is currently under redevelopment and will be open for September 2007.

GOFFS, Ireland – founded in 1866, named after Robert Goff, the first official auctioneer. It moved premises to a new 78-acre site in 1974 at County Kildare.

TATTERSALLS, England – founded in 1766 by Richard Tattersall. The main auction site is in Newmarket, with a second sales ring at Old Fairyhouse, Ireland. Tattersalls are the European leaders in the bloodstock industry, and still price horses in guineas, the gold coin from 1663.

The breeding industry continues to grow throughout the world, especially in Ireland, where they have produced nine of the last 15 English Derby winners with the likes of Sinndar, Galileo, High Chaparral, and North Light since the Millennium. Meanwhile in America during 2005, the world record for a yearling at auction was smashed when John Magnier, Michael Tabor, and Derrick Smith paid $16 million dollars for a son of Forestry. The previous record was $13.1 million dollars for Seattle Dancer in 1985, but The Green Monkey now carries the burden of the new record price tag, and will be stabled at Churchill Downs, Kentucky.

Above
The gavel goes down on a world record sale for a 2-year-old thoroughbred after the winning bid of $16 million, 2006.

Far left
Bidding in progress at Tattersall's horse auctions in Knightsbridge, London in 1938.

Left
Richard Tattersall, founder of Tattersall's auctioneers, 1766.

Right
Jockeys being weighed-in and horses being rubbed-down, 1850.

The art of handicapping, along with handicap races themselves, have been in existence for over 150 years, and are designed to give horses of various ability an equal chance of winning.

For example, if an average man were asked to run against the Olympic Champion on the track, the superior athlete would win comfortably off level weights. But if the Olympic Champion were to be allocated a rucksack full of rocks to carry on his back, the race would become a lot closer as the weight would inevitably slow the athlete down. This process, in effect, is what is known as handicapping in the equine world, with superior horses given more weight to carry in handicap races. Over half the events run in Great Britain are such races.

The decision to allocate specific weights to certain horses is determined by a team of ten handicappers from the British Horseracing Board, whose job it is to monitor every horse's performance. Each horse is given an official rating according to his or her level of ability, and this figure is represented in pounds. In order to gain a handicap mark, the handicapper

CHAPTER 10 HANDICAPPING

must be able to assess the horse on ability shown. On the Flat a horse must have run at least three times, unless it has won within its first two races. The horse is then allocated a rating from 0 upwards, with the best horses – Derby runners – earning ratings around the 120 mark on the Flat. The scale in National Hunt is obviously bigger, as larger horses carry bigger jockeys, and the scale runs from 0 into the 170s, with handicaps open to horses with a rating of 90 to 150.

The very top handicaps on the Flat, however, are only open to horses with a ceiling rating of 115, so a horse running in one of these races from an official rating of 114 against a horse with a rating of 100, would have to concede 14lbs, or a stone, in weight carried.

After the race has taken place, the handicapper will then assess how the horse ran, and decide whether to alter its rating. If the horse rated 114 were to win or even be placed in that race, the handicapper may decide to raise him a few more pounds, meaning the horse would no longer be eligible to run in handicaps in the future as it would have risen above the maximum rating allowed of 115. At the other end of the scale, the horse with a rating of 100 may have run badly as a result of being in decline, and the handicapper may drop him a few pounds to 98. This also presents an opportunity for the horse to run in lower grade handicap, say with a ceiling rating of 100.

Right
The offices of the Jockey Club in the High Street, Newmarket.

Below
Major E H Eggerton, official handicapper to the Jockey Club, 1889.

The handicapper will use a weight scale for different distances to guide him as to how much alteration should be made to an official rating, which will read something like the following:

FLAT

5-6f	3lb per length
7-8f	2½lb per length
9-11f	2lb per length
12f+	1½lb per length

NATIONAL HUNT

2m	2lb per length
2m 4f	1½lb per length
3m	1lb per length
3m+	½lb per length

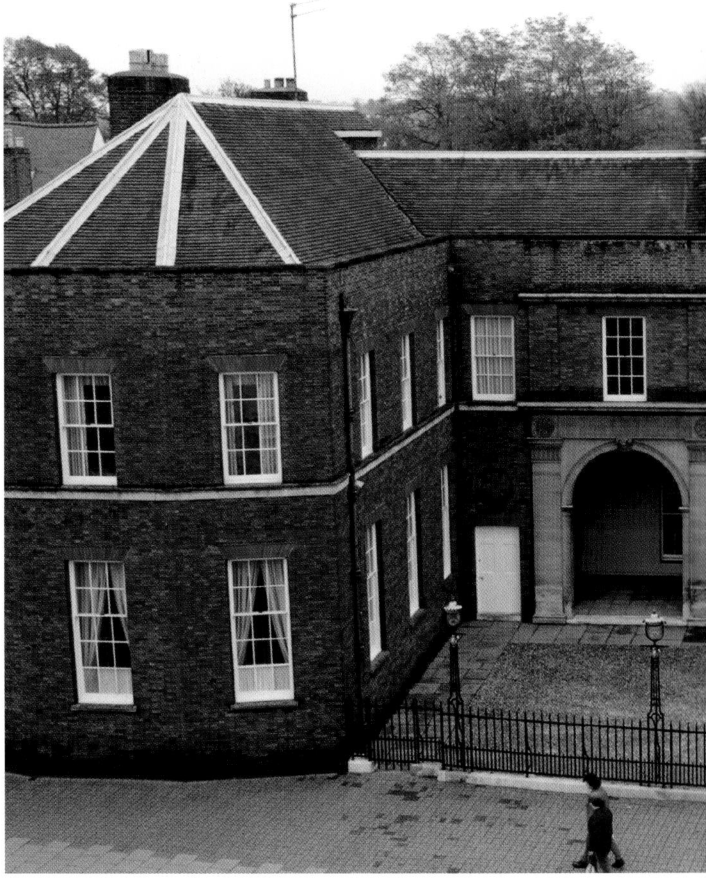

There is a whole range of handicaps open for horses to be entered, from the poor races for individuals rated in the 50s – selling handicaps – right up to the best ones for horses rated no higher then 115. There is also a maximum and minimum weight scale in handicaps for both codes, with the top-weight on the Flat of 10 stone down to the bottom-weight of 7 stone 12lbs, and in National Hunt it ranges from 12 stone down to 10. A horse entered in a handicap whose rating suggests it should carry less than the minimum weight is therefore forced into running from 'out of the handicap', meaning it still has to carry the minimum load.

The new official ratings are altered once a week by the team at the BHB, and are then forwarded to Weatherbys – an administrative racing body – by Tuesday morning, where, nowadays, they are stored on computer as opposed to the ledgers of past days. If a horse runs quickly before its new rating is allocated, then it will usually be asked to carry a penalty which is included in the race title, and can vary from 3lb to 7lb. One of the advantages that can be gained by connections of an improving horse shooting up the ratings quickly is to run it two or three times within a short spell, as it

can only carry the one penalty before the handicapper reassess it.

Two-year-olds have their own exclusive handicaps, called nurseries, which they race in before joining the handicapping ranks as three-year-olds. These nursery handicaps are only run from the middle of July onwards, a point in the season at which the handicapper can get to grips with all juvenile form. As the majority of juveniles will still be improving, and with just a handful of runs for each individual on offer, the handicapper will use other horses' ratings it has come up against as a benchmark.

When a horse reaches three, it is allowed to race in handicaps either against its own age group, or up against its elders. In the latter scenario, a three-year-old is given a weight allowance for racing against older and more mature horses, and the concession is decided by the WFA – weight-for-age scale. This was first designed by Admiral Rous, a member of the Jockey Club back in 1855, and has been amended throughout the years.

There a few exceptions to the overall handicapping rule, and in recent times the BHB handicappers have decided upon allocating separate handicap ratings to Irish National Hunt horses, mainly hurdlers, against the ones given to them in their native country. This sliding scale is to reflect the different age-for-weight systems, resulting in the best Irish hurdlers having to carry up to 9lb more over in England.

The Grand National also receives individual treatment, as runners are not automatically entered in the race on their official ratings. Britain's senior jumps handicapper, Phil Smith of the BHB, frames the weights for the world-famous handicap based on other relevant factors, such as the horse's form around Aintree, and ability to stay the distance. But the main reason for handicap marks to be tinkered with in this particular race is to encourage the better horses to run, as history suggests it is very difficult for a horse to carry huge weights in the Grand National. The weights for this race are now more compressed, giving the best horses more chance of winning without giving away lumps of weight, which is what handicapping is all about.

Below
The scale of weight-for-age has not changed in 100 years.

WEIGHT-FOR-AGE SCALE TABLE

Distance	Years of Age	Jan Feb	Mar Apr	May	Jun	Jul	Aug	Sep	Oct	Nov Dec
Half mile	2	–	–	–	–	–	105	108	111	114
	3	117	119	121	123	125	126	127	128	129
	4	130	130	130	130	130	130	130	130	130
	5 & up	130	130	130	130	130	130	130	130	130
Six furlongs	2	–	–	–	–	–	102	105	108	111
	3	114	117	119	121	123	125	126	127	128
	4	129	130	130	130	130	130	130	130	130
	5 & up	130	130	130	130	130	130	130	130	130
One mile	2	–	–	–	–	–	–	96	99	102
	3	107	111	113	115	117	119	121	122	123
	4	127	128	127	126	126	126	126	126	126
	5 & up	128	128	127	126	126	126	126	126	126
One and a quarter mile	2	–	–	–	–	–	–	–	–	–
	3	101	107	111	113	116	118	120	121	122
	4	125	127	127	126	126	126	126	126	126
	5 & up	127	127	127	126	126	126	126	126	126
One and a half miles	2	–	–	–	–	–	–	–	–	–
	3	98	104	108	111	114	117	119	121	122
	4	124	126	126	126	126	126	126	126	126
	5 & up	126	126	126	126	126	126	126	126	126
Two miles	2	96	102	106	109	112	114	117	119	120
	3	124	126	126	126	126	125	125	124	124
	4	126	126	126	126	126	125	125	124	124

Right
Gentlemen on horseback clamour to place their bets for the forthcoming race, c1800.

It could be argued that without betting, there would be no horse racing. Betting is one of the main ingredients in the recipe which holds the horse racing industry together, and sources back hundreds of years to when owners put up stakes in matches involving their horses. That was when the first betting seeds were sewn, and have now grown into a multi-million pound industry throughout the world. In Hong Kong for instance, betting turnover on horse racing with bookmakers in 2005 was just over £8 billion.

Bookmakers have been operating in Britain since the late 18th century, with the first odds being offered on-course at Newmarket in 1790, and in 1842, the first cry of the odds being called was heard on Newmarket Heath emanating from a certain Mr. Pedley who went on to win the Derby in 1847 with Cossack, ridden by S. Templeman. In the 1850s the first betting ring (the area where bookmakers operate) was formalised at Doncaster. Betting shops were up and running in the first half of the 19th century, before the Betting Houses Act closed them in 1853, because they were seen to be "mischievous".

CHAPTER 11 BETTING

It was another hundred years before betting shops were re-opened, during which time an opportunity was presented for illegal bookmakers to trade, with 'bookie's runners' visiting workplaces to accept and settle bets. These runners would be sent around offices and factories by bike or taxi, collecting bets from punters. Illegal bookmakers were in a comfortable position as there was no tax to declare, although the odd policeman might have to be paid for exercising discretion regarding their activities.

This was common practice until 1961, when betting shops were once again legalised and open to the public, leading to betting turnover soaring. This inevitably encouraged the introduction of taxation from the government, which came into effect during 1966. The result was a drop in turnover once again.

However, betting on horse racing in Britain was to witness a massive boom period in the eighties, ignited by the introduction of television screens in betting shops in 1987, replacing the audio commentary. Betting shops were also allowed to install fruit machines at this time, and punters began flocking back to the bookmakers.

The nineties, however, saw the National Lottery along with scratch cards introduced, stealing a slice of the major bookmakers' horse racing clients. Their troubles worsened when smaller bookmakers started offering tax-free betting abroad, but they were assisted in their fight to keep customers

BETTING

Above
Bookmakers taking bets at Royal Ascot, 1878.

Above middle
Punters entering a Dave Gilbert bookmaker's in London, 1961.

Above far right
A bookie performs tic-tac, a sign language used to convey odds information between course bookmakers, 1948.

in October 2001. It was then that the government abolished tax, heralding an explosion in betting on horses in Britain.

The period of tax-free betting also coincided with technological innovations allowing punters to place bets over the phone, on the Internet, on a mobile phone, or through an interactive television. This breakthrough has also affected part of the sport's heritage on-course, as the bookmakers' code of communicating with each other – 'tic-tac' – has gradually declined, with mobile phones replacing the old arm-waving style. The old blackboards and chalk, used to display the bookmaker's odds, have also been exchanged for electronic display screens.

Modern-day betting shops would be unrecognisable to punters from the sixties and seventies, as they have now relieved themselves of the shabby image from the past and are aimed towards a new breed of customer. The shops now aim to create a casino- type atmosphere, with transparent front-windows, improved air-conditioning, refreshments, comfortable fittings, digital screens, and fixed odds terminals. The latter especially allows punters to bet instantly on pre-recorded and virtual racing, and contributes highly towards the record turnover figures regularly being produced by leading bookmakers.

Betting on horse racing abroad has also gradually become more popular over the years, with live races now being beamed into households, enabling people to bet until midnight with English bookmakers by phone or Internet.

However, one of the major changes in recent years has been the introduction of betting exchanges. Introduced via the Internet in 2000, the betting exchanges allow an individual to play the role of bookmaker or punter, setting odds for others without the involvement of bookmakers. The money is deposited before a race with the company running the exchange – like a broker – and then paid out after the event.

The exchanges also present the opportunity to back a horse during the race – 'in-running' – which has recently been duplicated by Ladbrokes in their shops in an attempt to keep up with the ever-changing pulse of the betting industry.

The exchanges, however, have also brought controversy, as they allow individuals who maybe associated with a horse to lay it to lose, an opportunity not open before in Britain. This has forced racing's governing bodies to tighten up security procedures, a long-overdue measure which has helped keep the image of the sport clean.

ODDS AND BETS

Over the years, a system has evolved whereby the odds bookmakers offer for a horse are based on the probability of it winning. That probability is represented by a percentage, which is then converted into a price using an odds-compiler's table. A horse that has a 50 per cent chance of winning will be priced at evens, a horse with a 40 per cent chance will be priced at 6-4, and so on. Different types of bets have also varied in the history of the sport, so that nowadays there are some standard bets.

WIN – Predicting the single outcome of a race, where the horse must finish first. A stake of £1 to win on a horse at odds of 2-1 would return £3. Odds of 2-1 mean £1 multiplied by two, plus the original stake of £1.

PLACE – Predicting that a horse will not win, but finish placed under the following rules:

In races of five to seven runners, a placed horse must finish in the first two.

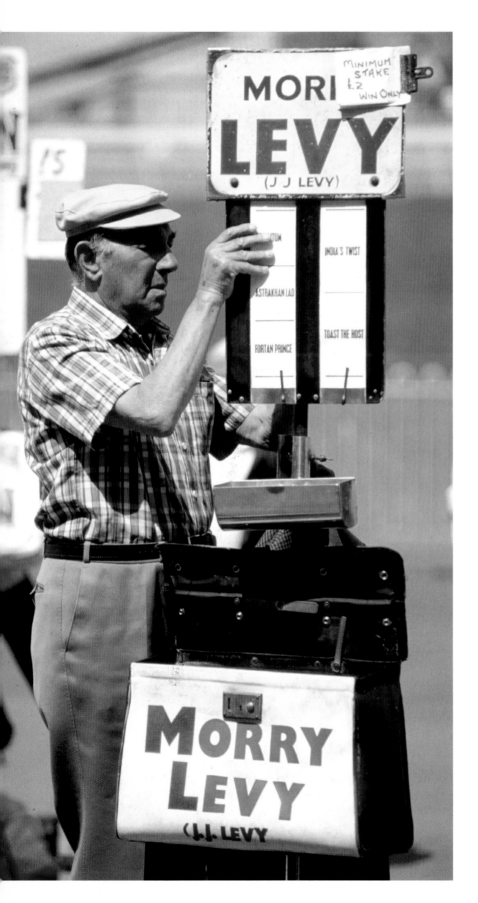

In races of eight or more runners, a placed horse must finish in the first three.

In handicap races of 16 runners or more, a placed horse must finish in the first four.

EACH-WAY – A combination of the above bets, resulting in two stakes. One stake is for the horse to win and the other stake is for it to be placed.

DOUBLE – A double includes two separate races. The amount won on the first race is then carried forward to the second race. A treble includes a third race, and an accumulator involves four or more races.

YANKEE – Four horses are selected in 11 bets covering doubles, trebles and an accumulator.

FORECAST – Predicting the two horses to finish first and second in a race. A straight forecast involves having them in the correct order – Horse A to beat Horse B – and a reverse forecast covers them either way.

PLACEPOT – Predicting horses to be placed in the first six races on a card. Any number of horses can be selected in each race, increasing the amount of bets in a permutation.

JACKPOT – Predicting the winner in the first six races on a selected card of the day, again with permutations.

ANTE-POST – Predicting the winner of a race well in advance of the event taking place, offering a punter the chance to benefit from big odds, such as betting on a horse at Christmas to win the Grand National in April at 66-1. The downside is that stakes are lost if the horse does not make it to the start.

THE TOTE – Betting on the Tote, or Totalisator, is simply pool betting. The money staked on a race is split between the winning tickets, which can sometimes outperform the odds offered by bookmakers.

Early bookmaking was not controlled and was open to many abuses. It was in 1865 that Pierre Oller, who ran a perfume shop in Paris, introduced this type of gambling to ensure that pay-outs were fairer and the influence of corrupt bookmakers less obtrusive. Oller sold tickets on horses in a race, kept a handling charge and divided the spoils between the winning ticket holders. The system became the legalised form of betting in France by 1887 and took the name Pari-mutuel, which has nothing to do with Paris but is a literal

Far left
A Bookmaker at Sandown, 1989.

Left
Modern day betting shop.

translation of mutual wager. 40 years later Sir Winston Churchill, as chancellor, allowed the system to be the legal form of betting in the United Kingdom.

At about the same time, the system arrived in the United States, but a young engineer by the name of Henry Strauss was much perturbed by the fact that he was given a much-reduced pay-out after a bet in Maryland.

Together with some fellow engineers, he developed a machine that not only calculated all the odds and winnings, but also displayed them on a large board for the benefit of the punters. Strauss had combined with other engineers to develop the system under the title of the American Totalisator Co., with the first public use of the machine taking place at the Pimlico track in 1930.

This form of pool betting is popular in countries such as France, America and Hong Kong.

SPREAD BETTING – A modern invention, allowing punters to buy or sell their predictions, meaning the more right they are, the more they win, and the more wrong they are, the more they lose. This makes spread betting a lot more volatile than fixed odds betting. An individual can buy or sell certain trades in a horse race such as the length of the winning distances over an entire race card, match betting between just two horses, and the number of favourites to win.

IMAGES SUPPLIED COURTESY OF:

GETTY IMAGES
101 Bayham Street, London NW10AG

EMPICS
www.empics.com

DESIGN & ARTWORK: Kevin Gardner • **PROJECT EDITOR:** Vanessa Gardner

IMAGE RESEARCH: Ellie Charleston & Kevin Gardner • **EDITING:** Ralph Dellor and Stephen Lamb

WRITTEN BY: David Myers